LA EMIGRACION Y EL EXILIO

EN

LA LITERATURA HISPANICA DEL SIGLO VEINTE

COLECCION POLYMITA

EDICIONES UNIVERSAL. Miami, Florida, 1988

MYRON I. LICHTBLAU
EDITOR

LA EMIGRACION Y EL EXILIO EN LA LITERATURA HISPANICA DEL SIGLO VEINTE

P.O. Box 450353 (Shenandoah Station)
Miami, Florida 33145 U.S.A.

Library of Congress Catalog Card No.: 87-81465

I.S.B.N.: 0-89729-445-9

A la memoria de
Lino Novás Calvo (1905-1983);
A Herminia Novás Calvo,
quienes convirtieron el exilio
en un triunfo.

CONTENIDO

LA EXPERIENCIA ARGENTINA: PARA CONMEMORAR EL CENTESIMO ANIVERSARIO DEL NACIMIENTO DE RICARDO GUIRALDES (1886-1986)

LA EXPERIENCIA HISPANOAMERICANA

Prefacio

Estos ensayos fueron presentados originalmente en un simposio celebrado en la Universidad de Syracuse el 24 y 25 de octubre de 1986, con el título "Emigration and Exile: Remembrance and Return to Origins in Twentieth-Century Hispanic Literature." El simposio fue patrocinado por el Department of Foreign Languages and Literatures y por el Centro de Estudios Hispánicos. Este evento habría sido imposible sin la ayuda y generoso apoyo financiero de muchos individuos e instituciones. Quedo profundamente agradecido a la Spanish Cultural Office, al New York State Council For The Humanities, a la Embajada Argentina, y, dentro de la Universidad de Syracuse, a La Casa Latinoamericana, la Graduate Student Organization, Foreign and Comparative Studies, el Humanities Ph.D. Program, la Division of International Programs Abroad, y University College. Y por último, debo dar las gracias a los otros miembros del comité organizador—Jaime Ferrán, Kathleen Newman, y Daniel Testa—por sus ideas y ardua labor en la realización de este simposio.

M.I.L.

INTRODUCCION

EXILE AND LITERATURE: A NATURAL CONVERGENCE

Myron Lichtblau
Syracuse University

This symposium on "Emigration and Exile: Remembrance and Return to Origins in Twentieth-Century Hispanic Literature" started out as a conference to commemorate the centennial anniversary of the birth of the Argentine Ricardo Güiraldes (1886-1928), whose classic novel *Don Segundo Sombra* is a paean to the disappearing gaucho of the 1920s. The general theme of our conference was to be the*criollista* novel, the novel of the land that distinguished Spanish American fiction in the period 1920-40. But in committee deliberations, thanks to the greater wisdom of Daniel Testa, we decided to broaden the scope of the conference to include all manifestations of alienation, uprootedness, separation, and exclusion from the cultural nucleus of one's country. The Argentine gaucho suffered this kind of inner exile, this feeling of excision in his own land, and so did Santos Luzardo as he tried to recover his ancestral lands usurped by the predatory Doña Bárbara in the novel that bears her name. And so too did Arturo Cova and Clemente Silva in *La vorágine* as they wandered through the inhospitable Colombian jungle like unwanted outsiders defying the inexorable forces of nature.

The concept of remembrance and nostalgia are inherent in all forms of exilic literature, just as it must have been in the mind of Güiraldes as he mythologized the gaucho and created a legendary hero figure of an ideal gaucho who could never have really existed. Remembrance and nostalgia are seen in the *Comentarios reales* of the Inca Garcilaso de la Vega, perhaps the first Spanish American literary exile. Remembrance and nostalgia are present too in a mestizo's dolorous account of his childhood experiences in an Indian environment in José María Arguedas' semi-autobiographical novel *Los ríos profundos*.

The trauma of the Civil War divided Spain and created a vast literature in exile. But those who chose to remain were also exiles in a nation oppressed and repressed. A decade before, Miguel de Unamuno likewise became a victim of political tyranny and suffered exile. Absence from one's country and the ambivalent longing to return produce an anguished if not tortured feeling of loss of identity, of non-belonging, rationalized at times, masked at other times, but ever present and alive. But Juan Goytisolo writes from within Spain of a similar inner exile in *Juan sin tierra* and *Señas de identidad*, and Juan Benet harbors analogous emotions when he writes *Volverás a región*. Paul Ilie, in his pioneering book *Literature and Inner Exile*, comments on the two Spains, what he calls "España peregrina" and "España solariega": "Consequently, we may say with accuracy that resident Spain found itself banished from the spiritual presence of the emigrés and condemned to an exile in a cultural desert. Both Spains were afflicted by withdrawal and exclusion, the two sides of the same exile."

Spanish America, which was once the refuge of those exiled from Spain, in recent years has seen its own writers seek the freedom of other lands, including Spain. If Spain suffered one single convulsive event in 1936, Spanish America, subdivided politically as it is but with a common language, has suffered many convulsive events, each one pushing writers and intellectuals over national borders. The exile literature that emerges outside of Castro's Cuba is separate from but not independent of the resident literature. So is the literature of the Argentine emigrés; so is the literature of the Chilean emigrés. But the voices of those who endure geographical exile are no more painful and intense than the voices of those who suffer emotional banishment in their own country and record their experiences in poetry and fiction.

We should dedicate this symposium to the memory of Lino Novás Calvo, Cuba's great short story writer, who suffered exile three times, first from his native Galicia at the age of seven, then from his adopted Cuba as he covered the Spanish scene in the thirties as a correspondent, and then again from Cuba in 1960 when he came to New York as a frustrated and disillusioned writer. Lino honored Syracuse University with his presence on campus as professor of Latin American literature from 1968 until his retirement in 1974. Perhaps the fulfillment he experienced here at Syracuse mitigated the pain of his exile. Some of the themes presented at this symposium touch the very anguish Lino felt as a man and as a writer. He would have enjoyed these essays.

REMEMBRANCE AND CREATIVE NOSTALGIA IN JUAN GOYTISOLO
(and the Misplaced Presence of Rousseau)

Randolph D. Pope
Washington University

"This Discourse is not concerned with those metaphysical subtleties that have spread to all departments of Literature, and of which the Programs of Academies are not always free: it is concerned, rather, with one of those truths that affect the happiness of mankind" (2). With these words Rousseau begun in 1750 the preface of his *Discourse* on the question proposed by the Academy of Dijon, "Whether the restoration of the Sciences and Arts has contributed to the purification of morals." The question is timeless and Terry Eagleton's book *The Function of Criticism* is just one recent example that echoes Rousseau, including in its preface this statement: "The argument of this book is that criticism today lacks all substantive social function" (7). Both Rousseau and Eagleton believe there is something to be said that could influence the actual way in which readers live. Writers who wish to prescribe a better way of life and that normally describe dourly the evil of present times can be called moralists. Their aim is to unsettle the readers' confidence in their nests, to show the fabrications where common beliefs are grounded, and to shatter with fictions the factitious ideals and needs of society. Such a writer is Juan Goytisolo, who has consistently deplored the rigidity, provincialism, and repression of Spanish society, as well as the triviality of the global shopping mall. The strategy of his rhetoric is similar to Rousseau's and of a third writer I will introduce later in this paper. I believe that the kinship has not been detected nor the consequences explored and my aim here is only to broach a subject that merits further and collective thought.

To criticize the present times an alternative image is needed, a utopic society in the future or a golden age in the past. Here is where Rousseau deployed his sacred icons, men who did not know yet how to hide their true being, a state where property was unthought of, the primal festival next to the watering hole, and a brand-new poetic language. "One cannot reflect on morals, without taking delight in recalling the image of simplicity of the first times. It is a fair shore, adorned by the hands of nature alone, toward which one forever turns one's eyes, and from which one feels oneself moving away with regret" (18). Rousseau clearly acknowledged that his imagined origin of humanity was possibly only a literary creation, the point being that ultimately the convincing force of his argument relied on his readers recognizing in themselves some traces of a better original self: "it is no light undertaking to disentangle what is original from what is artificial in man's present Nature, and to know accurately a state which no longer exists, which perhaps never did exist, which probably never will exist" (130). When Juan Goytisolo structures his three novels, *Señas de identidad*, *La reivindicación del Conde don Julián*, and *Juan sin Tierra*, as examinations of the past, the search is for an uncontaminated root of writing. Alvaro Mendiola, in *Señas de identidad*, has returned to Spain and during three days of passion sifts through his past to understand his present dejection, symbolized by his failing heart. He lives in "un mundo otoñal y caduco" (11), he is part of a "degenerada raza" (18) and a leaf in the "aborrecido árbol genealógico" (55). In this novel the sin is found in the ancestor who became rich by exploiting slaves in Cuba, whose benefits Alvaro still enjoys, while sharing the need to expiate the tainted leisure that allows him to study and make movies: "el amo remoto —responsable tuyo en el moroso sucederse de las generaciones" (14). Intimations of purity are found in the rebellious nature of youth, in sex, in the peasants who when they work collectively illustrate "la unidad recobrada del hombre" (132), and in the fishermen that shame Alvaro with their true solidarity that he can only supplant by handing them a few old bills. The core of the novel if forcibly and clearly expressed:

> Las mutilaciones remotas infligidas a tu cuerpo por el orgullo racial de unos paisanos pervertidos por sus dogmas y aquellas otras, más recientes, obra de tu bisabuelo traficante (esclavas ofrecidas a su capricho y placer, hombres reducidos a la mísera condición de instrumentos de trabajo) las asumías tú, en tu carne y espíritu, como cosecha necesaria (expiación tal vez) del mal hosco y cerril que sembraran en vida. Gracias a los malditos y parias de siempre (gitanos, negros, árabes instintivos y bruscos), habías logrado fraguar en ti, por unos minutos, la antigua unidad perdida hacia lo que tu impulso rebelde tendía, por encima de preceptos y leyes, con irreductible nostalgia. (56)

Remembering, as though overheard by an analyst, may restore the mutilated organs to its full functions. The impulse for this painful operation comes from that unsettling call home from the intelligence, the nostos and nous of nostalgia. The model is not only Christ, who assumes the sins of the world, but also those human beings who remain uncorrupted by civilization, in touch with their instincts and passions. This is where our third writer comes in, Sigmund Freud, who in 1927, in *The Future of an Illusion*, worried about civilization and doubted its value for the happiness of humanity. Freud developed his thoughts further in *Civilization and its Discontents*, published in 1930. By this time he believed that next to libido or Eros, there existed in the human being an instinct of destruction or Thanatos, and that the story of humanity had to be considered a struggle between the constructive forces of love and the destructive efforts of death. Civilization, to survive, constrains sexual instinct and human aggressiveness, using as an instrument the mind's capacity for internalizing prohibition and transforming real or imagined violations into guilt. Carping back to Rousseau, Freud affirms that "aggressiveness was not created by property," but instead "it reigned almost without limit in primitive times" (67). His verdict is tentatively pessimistic: "perhaps we may also familiarize ourselves with the idea that there are difficulties attaching to the nature of civilization which will not yield to any attempt at reform" (70). Goytisolo will reach a similar conclusion and consider life strapped by the "binomio creación-descreación" in a "universo mal hecho" (*Coto vedado*, 67). In *Reivindicación* it appears that the destruction of Spanish myths would be enough to restore the country and, therefore, the individual to integrity, to their original destiny. This is only a convex image of Imperial Spain. Debasing Queen Isabella, committing partial suicide by condemming himself as a child to the gallows, does not appease the narrator who is incessantly invading Spain in his mind, but also is invaded by a degrading society in which he must live: "lo sabes, lo sabes: mañana será otro día, la invasión recomenzará" (240). The agent of the last verb, the new beginning, "recomenzará," is not the narrator, but the instinct of destruction that needs incessantly to create a clearing in the constantly growing stuffiness of civilization. Rousseau looked to the primitive human being as his model, Freud to the newborn child, Goytisolo considers briefly peasants and fishermen, but settles on the Arabs, whose repression has allowed Spanish civilization and its discontents to flourish. That these three writers are presenting radical and unwelcome news can explain the capacity the three have had to irritate their readers: they question the very core of our activity as readers, as civilized people. By becoming civilized, we deteriorate (Rousseau), we repress our deeper instincts thereby guaranteeing our unhappiness (Freud), and we lose contact with our true self joining the oppressors and hypocrites (Goytisolo).

I do not believe these conceptions of reality are offered to amuse us. There is urgency in them, a desire to convert, to illuminate, and to change our way of living: we need to be healed from the wounds inflicted upon us by civilization. Here is where the strategy of these three writers gets even closer and more intriguing. If they wish to prove the truth of a concept that is repugnant to our superficial common sense, they have to provide an unquestionable case based on a well known example. Thus, all three turn to themselves, and their writing slides into autobiography, even if resisting its full tug, since they wish to be exemplary of humanity and not just of Jean-Jacques, Sigmund, or Juan.[1] They will derive their authority from their lives, and this is exactly the way in which most readers will have it. The personal attacks against the three of them are too well known for me to need document them here. Goytisolo remembers in *Coto vedado* that his philosophy teacher in high school attacked the "afeminamiento de Rousseau" (124). What matters is that this is not misdirected argumentation *ad hominem*, as Goytisolo writes misplacing Rousseau and himself, but a necessary development of their thought. A moralist must illustrate the truth of his message with his own life, or his writings are just empty and trivial exercises in rhetoric. The thinly veiled autobiographical nature of the character Alvaro Mendiola is brought to the open when by an inspired typographical error in *Señas de identidad* where it should read "dijo" we are startled by "dije" (95). Goytisolo moves closer to himself in *Juan sin Tierra*, precisely by inverting the model of life he had been offered as Alvarito in *Señas de identidad*. In that novel the narrator remembers his childhood: "Tú admirabas, celoso, la sincronizada precisión de aquellas vidas cimeras que tan cruelmente contrastaban con la rutina y vacuidad de la tuya, soñando, a falta de la suspirada aparición, en la maligna enfermedad que pudiera ponerte a prueba o en el codiciable y espectacular martirio" (24). A transposition happens in *Juan sin Tierra*: the narrator does not imitate the saints, but the rebels, Lawrence of Arabia, Ibn Turmeda, Pere de Foucald and Kavafis, but the same principle is operative. His attempt to be reborn as an African god fails, his identifications do not stick: there is always a defect, a lack: that lack is simply individual existence that has to prove its value only as itself. It is not surprising, therefore, that Goytisolo's next book is one of the best among the few true autobiographies written in Spain. *Coto vedado* turns at last to Goytisolo himself to prove there how family and nation have corrupted his original pure self, recovered only after a descent into darkness.

Freud became his best client, split between the analyst and the analyzand, unable to live or dream without a proliferation of notes trying to harness precisely what was revealed as the unpredictable and unknowable self. He invented his own opponents in his writings, most notably in *The Future of an Illusion*. Rousseau wrote not only the *Confessions*, but at the end of his life the curious *Dialogues ou Rousseau juge de Jean-Jacques*, where a Frenchman and a character named Rousseau set out to find out who Jean-Jacques really is, and they divide their work, one of them reading all Rousseau's works, while the other visits the man.[2] The dialogic narrator of Goytisolo's trilogy and of parts of the autobiography shows this same split caused by becoming his own example.

The moralists have seen into the irredeemable nature of society and the self, and they wish to warn us by convincingly exposing their own selves and leading a life that authorizes their writing. (Does it make any difference how Benet, Cela or Marsé live? They are not moralists, so they are under no obligation to exemplify what they preach, if they do preach at all. On the other hand, this feature is what makes it reasonable that Sartre has conferred sainthood on Genet.) The problem for Rousseau, Freud, and Goytisolo is that this courageous and unusual investigation of the self leads to uncomfortable revelations hard to accomodate. Let us compare briefly two anecdotes, one from the *Confessions* the other from *Coto vedado*.

Rousseau had recently converted from Protestantism to Catholicism when he began working as a lackey at the house of a rich widow, Mme. de Vercellis, who soon died of cancer. When the inventory was taken, a small ribbon was found missing and was later discovered in Rousseau's room. He blamed a young servant, Marion, an attractive woman he admits to have liked. Mme de Vercellis' nephew, Count de la Roque, decided after an investigation to fire both Rousseau and Marion, affirming that the guilty conscience of the culprit would be enough punishment. He was right:

> J'en emportai les long souvenirs du crime et l'insupportable poids des remords dont au bout de quarante ans ma conscience est encore chargée, et dont l'amer sentiment, loin de s'affaiblir, s'irrite a mesure que je vieillis. Qui croirait que la faute d'un enfant put avoir des suites aussi cruelles? C'est de ces suites plus que probables que mon coeur ne saurait se consoler. J'ai peut-etre fait périr dans l'opprobre et dans la misere une fille aimable,

> honnete, estimable, et qui surement valait beaucoup mieux que moi. (91)

Marion became for Rousseau a veritable nightmare that concentrated for him in a bitter image "des innocents persécutés" (93). The fact that private property was involved, as well as dissimulation, may have oriented his later thought. The origin of his deception had to be displaced from his own evil behavior to the corruption of a system and of society. In *Coto vedado* there are two stories that correspond to Rousseau's experience. First, when Franco's troops invade the town where the Goytisolo family has retired during the Civil War, Juan's father decides to fire the maid, who by her friendship with Republican soldiers had facilitated the life of the whole family:

> La sirvienta roja, barragana de comunistas y milicianos, acató la sentencia del tribunal sin decir palabra. Cabizbaja, sonrosada, fue a la habitación a recoger sus pobres enseres y cargarlos en un saco sin que ninguno de nosotros, sentados aún alrededor de los platos que un rato antes había guisado y servido, se levantara a despedirse de ella o darle alguna muestra de compasión. Con el saco a la espalda, resignada a su suerte, desapareció para siempre de nuestra vista. ¿Qué fue de ella en aquellos tiempos de control y represión inflexibles, en los que las detenciones arbitrarias y denuncias estaban a la orden del día?... Un sentimiento de bochorno retrospectivo me abruma al escribir estas líneas. Me parece increíble que yo, aun a mis ocho años, no hubiera experimentado remordimiento y vergüenza por aquel mezquino ajuste de cuentas. (77-78)

María, the servant of Goytisolo's family, is "sonrosada" just as Rousseau's Marion had "une fraicheur de coloris qu'on ne trouve que dans les montagnes" (92), in both cases underlining their healthy and natural sincerity as opposed to the corruption of more refined society. Later in *Coto vedado*, Goytisolo recalls how he used to pilfer change from his grandmother's purse with the impunity granted to him by her fading memory. He concludes: "Esta carencia chocante de sentido ético, fruto casi seguro de nuestra experiencia precoz de la guerra, nos iba a afectar de manera genérica a los cuatro hermanos: cada uno de nosotros, en un momento u otro de su vida, tendría que luchar duramente contra ella para imponer una norma de rectitud personal, en una larga y agotadora contienda de resultado dudoso" (107). That the memory of both anecdotes was scorching is seen when they reappear superposed at the end of *Reivindicación*, where Alvarito, forced to steal to please his sadistic lover, denounces the maid: "hay que denunciar a la criada, la vieja y abnegada fámula que, desde siempre, le sirve (te sirvió) con fidelidad y devoción: avisada por la madre, la policía practicará un minucioso registro y, bajo el colchón de la doméstica, encontrará las joyas y recuerdos de familia que previsoramente has puesto tú: ominosa visión de la desdichada mujer que deniega, gime, suplica, llora y desaparece finalmente en el hermético coche celular que la conduce en derechura al presidio" (226). A ribbon and small change, two fired maids, how important they came to be! Our moralist writers were not made by these events, they dwelt on them because they already had a superior call to confront their life and values. Freud marvels at this apparent paradox: that "the more virtuous a man is, the more severe and distrustful is its behavior, so that ultimately it is precisely those people who have carried saintliness furthest who reproach themselves with the worst sinfulness" (81). The ego strives always in vain to attain its rising ideal. At least, the creative recollection of the past will allow the writer to correct it, by introducing now the compassion missing then, not an insignificant activity.

True radical moralists are few, because they must endure public scrutiny and dare face in the open their most repressed secrets. Their autobiographical writings and their irritating, unsettling value, are as uncommon as they are lasting, because the problem of confronting an imperfect universe, a frustrating life, an unreliable and base ego are common experiences to us all, while few can face them squarely and bear their pain. That is why I may admire García Márquez's or Aldecoa's writings, but I admire Rousseau, Freud, and Juan Goytisolo.

[1] Goytisolo values Blanco White's autobiographical texts for the following, apparently paradoxical, reason: "El valor excepcional de su experiencia radica en el hecho de que cifra en sí la historia secreta de miles y miles de sus paisanos—una historia no escrita jamás, encerrada bajo siete llaves en el santuario de sus conciencias" (*Obra inglesa* 21). The epigraph to Goytisolo's "Presentación crítica" of Blanco White is a quote from Rousseau.

[2] I am grateful to my colleague James F. Jones for sharing with me his insightful readings of Rousseau's *Dialogues*, including the forthcoming article "On Names and Masks:, Rousseau as Renou."

Works Cited

Eagleton, Terry. *The Function of Criticism. From The Spectator to Post-Structuralism.* Thetford: Verso, 1984.

Freud, Sigmund. *Civilization and its Discontents.* Translated by James Strachey. New York: W. W. Norton, 1961.

Goytisolo, Juan. *Señas de identidad.* México: Joaquín Mortiz, 1966.

---. *Reivindicación del Conde don Julián.* Barcelona: Seix Barral, 1976. Primera edición: México: Joaquín Mortiz, 1970.

---. *Juan sin Tierra.* Barcelona: Seix Barral, 1975.

---. *Obra inglesa de José María Blanco White.* 3rd. ed. Barcelona: Seix Barral, 1982.

---. *Coto vedado.* Barcelona: Seix Barral, 1985.

Jones, James F. Jr. "The *Dialogues* as Autobiographical Truth." *Studies in Eighteenth-Century Culture* 14 (1985): 317-328.

Rousseau, Jean-Jacques. *Les confessions.* Paris: Garnier, 1964.

---. *The First and Second Discourses Together with the Replies to Critics and Essay on the Origin of Languages.* Translated and annotated by Victor Gourevitch. New York: Harper & Row, 1986.

INNER EXILE IN THE NOVELS AND TRAVELS OF CAMILO JOSE CELA

Robert Kirsner

University of Miami

From the very beginning, the writings of Camilo José Cela have been characterized by the underlying theme of spiritual self-banishment. In the expression of estrangement the author has identified with his characters. Indeed, particularly in his books of travel, Cela assumes the role of a wanderer in search of his soul. His own quest for identity through the palpation of the barren lands of Spain mirrors the situation of his novelistic characters as they grope for individual survival. Both, he and his literary creations appear to merge as they clamour for independence. Both, author and characters fail in their attempts to free themselves of shame and guilt, for in the art of Camilo José Cela the inevitable fate of human existence centers on relentless retribution.

Fifty years have passed since the advent of the Spanish Civil War. For the new generation of Spaniards, the collective fratricide of the years 1936-1939, is an annoying abstract event, which does not directly relate to their actuality. For Cela and his generation, on the other hand, Spanish life has not freed itself of the enduring feeling of culpability and humiliation. Especially for those participants who, like Cela, have felt betrayed by the false promises of their side, the winning side, existence has taken the form of intellectual withdrawal. Consequently, it is not surprising at all, that such spiritual alienation should have been transmitted to the *lives* the author has created. To be sure, each of his characters experiences a distinct form of isolation, but in the last analysis, none escapes the sensation of being an outcast. It is not a matter of reading into the characters, the apparent life of the author; we are dealing here with the inner experience of the artist as he labours in his literary laboratory. (Actually, in the realm of immediate experience, often misrepresented as "real life", Cela has enjoyed a good life even by standards of the most prosperous Western countries.)

Pascual Duarte, the first major character in the works of Camilo José Cela, embodies the salient qualities of the social outcast, the embattled misfit, whose only recourse is killing. Only through destruction can he palpate life. The flow of blood sustains him. Yet, his condition is self-imposed. He wills his fate. Let us remember that his protestations of innocence are made within the context of the social order which he had eschewed, but of which he is now an obligatory part, when he is already narrating the story of his family from a prison cell. While Pascual is acting out his destiny, there is no remorse, no exculpation. ("...una sensación de alivio me recorrió las venas... Podía respirar...") On the contrary, at the time of slaughter, Pascual revels in his independence, his liberation from society. "Podía respirar..." accentuates the repressive state of his social existence.

In *Pabellón de reposo* (1943), Cela's second novel, the state of inner exile is magnified by the presence of characters who, in the throes of their agonies, await death in a sanitorium for incurable tuberculars. Here the estrangement is not just from society, but in most cases, it is from one another. Consumed by shame and utter humiliation, destined to live out their remaining days amidst macabre surroundings of impending death, the patients rely on a poetic vision of beauty and love, in order to differentiate themselves, and thus feel distant from the healthy people who live *outside*, in the unfeeling city, which knows no silence.

> Los hombres sanos, los hombres que andan por la ciudad, que van y vienen a sus negocios, que se suben a los automóviles y se sientan en las cervecerías; los hombres a quienes ves a diario por las calles, nada saben de lo que es amar... nada saben de lo que es amar, porque nada saben tampoco del silencioso tránsito que se alarga, casi indefinidamente, como aquellos besos que tú y yo nos dábamos sentados al pie del árbol de tu jardín, para morir un día... [1]

In *La Colmena* (1951), hunger appears to be the motif which establishes the line of demarcation for the outcasts. However, the wall of separation between the penurious and the well-fed is a superficial one. Within both economic classes, distinguished solely by the abundance or lack of food, the novelistic characters tend to isolate themselves from one another. For example, without adequate nourishment but abounding with pride, Petrita, a poor servant who does not even have twenty-two *pesetas* to her name, succeeds in living out her momentary dream, free from the experience of Martín Marco, the starving poet whom she worships, and completely removed from the knowledge of her fiance. Her act of *nobility*, literarily speaking, her personal sacrifice, an act of social defiance for its time and place, remains as a gesture of concealed love, irreductibly hers. In the human beehive that is *La Colmena,* among the many characters that we meet, nearly three hundred of them, mostly all live in a state of individual isolation. Rare are the instances of social participation; there is a lack of collective understanding. The few moments of compenetration are fleeting and incomplete. By and large, each person, exemplified dramatically by the existence of Elvirita, the prostitute who goes to bed every night hungry, comforted only by undefined dreams and illusions, projects an anchoretic life. In the *Café* of doña Rosa, true to her profession, Elvirita puts on a good act as she haughtily pretends to live contentedly, without worries or cares.

Cela's books of travels, in which the author functions as character-narrator, reveal the same type of solipsism, but the expression of the chasmic human situation is frequently conveyed in direct acrimonious terms. At times, the literary imagery is virtually lost, and the projected reality emerges as a journalist factual commentary. Of particular significance is the first account of wanderlust, *Viaje a la Alcarria* (1948). In this intricate work, incongrous in its intent, we are confronted with a gallery of characters who peculiarly create realities which surpass the traditional limits of fanciful imagination. Thus, Estanislao de Kostka Rodríguez y Rodríguez, whose alias belies his assumed patrimony, believes himself to be the nephew and designated heir of the estate of the Viceroy of Peru. The document which purportedly gives evidence to such rights and privileges is kept in Rome since the beneficiary trusts no one but the Pope, himself.

> ¿Usted ha oído hablar del Virrey del Perú?
> —Sí, mucho.
> —Pues me dejó todos sus bienes. En el lecho de muerte llamó al notario y delante de él escribió en un papel: (Yo, don Jerónimo de Villegas y Martín, Virrey del Perú, lego todos mis bienes presentes y futuros a mi sobrino don Estanislao de Kostka Rodríguez, alias "el Mierda"). Me lo sé de memoria. El papelito está guardado en Roma porque yo ya estoy muy escarmentado, yo ya no me fío de nadie más que del Papa. [2]

The author as the "vagabond" in search of truth, desperate for some measure of understanding of Spanish life, discovers that each person lives within the constraints of his or her own dreams and illusions. Beyond the oppressiveness of a tyrannical government and pervading hunger, every person along the way appears to be a virtual island. Therefore, it is not too surprising to meet María, a maid who reads and who consequently becomes a quasi-romantic character. Contrarily, her sister, Elena, also a maid, is impervious to sentimentality; she reads nothing but newspapers. Another quaint inhabitant of the region known as La Alcarria, is Julio Vacas, alias Portillo, who imagines himself to be a collector of books. Don Julio gives the traveler two books on health because the latter appears to be quite pale and therefore in need of them. Don Julio is proud of his role as a benefactor and refuses at first, the two *pesetas* the traveler offers in return. In spite of dire economic need, the book collector chooses to follow the path of his inner demand for apparent nobility. Don Julio accepts the two *pesetas* only when it is made clear that they are being proffered as a gift. Then, he exclaims, "ese ya es otro cantar." Without a doubt, the two *pesetas* will mean the enjoyment of a good meal. We are in the aftermath of the Spanish Civil War.

The decades of the sixties, seventies, and eighties have also revealed a Camilo José Cela who continues to portray the inexorable loneliness of human existence. His enthusiasm for projecting individual detachment amid a throng of nameless people, who seem to live without purpose or direction has not abated, even though it has been considerably modified. The art of Cela has taken various forms, including the staging of an opera based on his *María Sabina* (1967), the tragic account of the life of a suspected thaumaturgist. *San Camilo 1936* (1969), particularizes the days immediately preceeding the outbreak of the Civil War. (" ...el hombre aprendió a hablar y más tarde a escribir y entonces descubrió que no hay dos hombres iguales, dos hombres que piensen lo mismo..."). As a corollary, we might add that neither are there two persons who have identical dreams. In *San Camilo 1936*, we experience the fragmentary movement of individual lives while dark clouds hover over them as they face the imminent arrival of an implacable war. Even in this moment of impending doom, when the entire nation is threatened with extinction, the individual continues to be obsessed with his/her own inner reality.

San Camilo, 1936 focuses on individual disillusionment. The dedicatory statement of the author pointedly indicates his intent.

> A los mozos del reemplazo del 37, todos perdedores de algo: de la vida, de la libertad, de la ilusión, de la esperanza, de la decencia.

> Y no a los aventureros foráneos, fascistas y marxistas, que se hartaron de matar españoles como conejos y a quienes nadie había dado vela en nuestro propio entierro. [3]

In the tradition of Galdós, who sought to exalt the role of the *insignificant* people in light of great historical events, Cela superimposes the projection of personal circumstances upon that of a national catastrophe. The unfolding of one life outweighs the importance of a nation. We have here inner individual history, not the banal account of those who "cut off heads" or those who have the distinction of having their heads cut off on the gallows.

> A Lorenzo Sosa lo atienden en el cine Velussia, está muy mal herido y se muere sin recobrar el conocimiento, de todos tendrás que hablar ya en tiempo pasado, la historia olvida a los hombres que no cortan cabezas o a quienes no cortan la cabeza en el patíbulo..."

If *San Camilo, 1936* deals with a variety of people, all with their own irreductible singular vital structures, *Rol de Cornudos* (1976), an irreverent, deliberately offensive book, centers its attention on one specific type of individual, that is to say, on the individual who has felt the arrows of social disgrace, the cuckold. Nonetheless, within the general designation of the shameful term, Cela uncovers distinct forms of attitudes and reactions. Even within the context of such a generic denomination, we are presented, however unpleasant the revelation may be, with a series of betrayed men who confront their situations quite differently; there are those who are placated with a *café con leche*, especially a large one, and a slice of good cake. Such a person experiences a sort of truce that frees him of wrath, if not of being a cuckold.

> *cornudo alborotador.* El que se desahoga con el escándalo que, sin pasar jamás a mayores, aboca en el armisticio que no le absuelve del cuerno pero sí de la ira. Es especie que se amansa con un café cortado y, aun mejor con un café con leche y una ensaimada rellena de cabello de ángel. [5]

The list of types, an individualization of the general classification, is quite extensive and recalls Cela's *Diccionario Secreto* (1971). In a sense, *Rol de Cornudos* constitutes an extension or amplification of his daring *Dictionary*.

Mazurca para dos muertos (1983), explores the lives of virtually forgotten people who live in Galicia. To facilitate the understanding of the language used, the author includes a Galician-Spanish (Castilian, to be exact) vocabulary. We meet in this book a number of characters who are distinguished by their individuality, their particular experience of life around them. *Mazurca para dos muertos* seems to combine the elements of a novel and a book of travel. To some extent, it represents the blend of the genres. And again, the Spanish Civil War, an irreductible motif in the works of Cela, always an integral part of Cela's imagery, serves as a frame of reference. The art of Cela is inexorably intertwined with the great event which became the prelude to World War II. Interestingly enough, the action in the book revolves around murder and vengeance; people's capacity for inhumanity does not cease to amaze the author—and his readers.

> Le voy a decir una cosa que todo el mundo sabe, usted, no, porque no para aquí, pero ya se la dejé medio dicha, recuerde: al muerto que mató a mi difunto lo desenterré, fui una noche hasta el camposanto de Carballino a robar el muerto, me lo traje para casa y eché la carroña al cerdo que después comí, los lacones por un lado, los chorizos con la cabeza por otro, y así hasta el final. Los Guxindes se alegraron y se callaron, y los Carroupos se cabrearon pero se callaron también porque si hablan, van detrás; es la ley de Dios...[6]

The horror of life, it might be said, surpasses the fear of death. Yet, within the cannibalistic society that is portrayed in *Mazurca para dos muertos*, we have the unfolding of individual life, which is virtually detached from murder and vengeance. On the contrary, we meet characters who are kind and loving. Benicia, for example, in the tradition of Maritornes, shares charitably her warmth and kindness. "Benicia guarda siempre calor, aunque haga frío; Benicia es una máquina de dar calor y gusto..." Moreover, she is polite and respectful. When she is with the priest, "Cerefino Furelo o sea Furelo Gamuzo", she addresses him with due courtesy at all times. "—¡Ay, don Cerefino, qué gusto me da usted! ¡Apriete, apriete...!" The list of characters is quite long, and each has a story, and an inner life of his/her own. Each lives within the walls of one's own soul. Ultimately, the social relationships or interdependencies only serve to intensify the individual's dreams and nightmares. As in all works of Cela, human destiny is projected as an irrevocable sentence of inner loneliness. Be it a murderer or an innocent victim, Pascual Duarte or the poor nameless cuckold; be it the vengeful widow, Rosalía Trasulfe, Cabuxa Tola, or the generous Benicia, all carry with them untransferable realities, which make of each, an isle of unending possibilities.

Notes

[1] Camilo José Cela, *Pabellón de reposo.* Ediciones Destino, S.L., Barcelona, Octubre 1952, (Segunda Edición). pp. 73 and 74.

[2] Camilo José Cela, *Viaje a la Alcarria.* Ediciones Destino, S.L., Barcelona, 1954. p. 110.

[3] Camilo José Cela, *San Camilo, 1936. (Vísperas, Festividad y Octava de San Camilo del Año 1936 en Madrid).* Alfaguara, Madrid-Barcelona, 1969. Dedicatory page.

[4] *Ibid.* p. 314.

[5] Camilo José Cela, *Rol de Cornudos.* Editorial Noguer, S.A. (Galería Literaria Contemporánea), Barcelona, 1976. p. 29.

[6] Camilo José Cela, *Mazurca para dos muertos.* Seix Barral (Biblioteca Breve), Barcelona, 1983. p. 47.

UNAMUNO IN EXILE: THE MAKING OF A NOVEL

Demetrios Basdekis
Suny, Oneonta

While Miguel de Unamuno had never really bothered to formulate, formalize, or systematize his theory of reading in any strictly rational or academic way, being as he was a self-declared enemy of the type of erudition rooted in the constructivism of some two thousand years of naturalism, being as he was the self-declared enemy of what his contemporary Edmund Husserl had denounced as the "natural standpoint" and its neat, geometric structuring through causality, we can nevertheless trace, scattered throughout the poetic, baroque, ontological hyperbole which is the recurring experiential pattern, or the so-called "coordinanting axis" of his complete works, a method of reading and novelizing for readers, whose fundamental structure is phenomenological. So much so, that we can reasonably conjecture today that Unamuno was indeed *the* great Peninsular pioneer, possibly the greatest European forerunner, of current reading theory, for he had not only anticipated, but had, additionally, thoroughly predated, if not by 1905, then certainly by 1914, not only Ortega y Gasset's phenomenological perception of reading, but all the reader-response criticism currently in vogue in North American academic circles. In addition to this unusual achievement, having had the formidable advantage of being a novelist himself, Unamuno was able to complement, to reinforce his theoretical sallies into the dialectical realm of author-reader-critic relationships by translating them into a more vital, dramatic fictional form, thus rendering his more abstract pronouncements concrete, extraordinarily convincing, judging by the enormous popularity of his novels. These novels can be viewed as fictional, or, perhaps counterfictional, companions of the many articles, prologues, epilogues, etc. in which he sporadically, yet persistently—sometimes obsessively—led his reader to a phenomenology of reading.

In retrospect, the explanation for this unusual achievement may, of course, seem fairly simple: What else might we have expected of a man who, as reader, was a paradigm; who spent his life reading; who lived to read; who read to live, and who read himself into the novel, into the novel of others, as well as into his own novel, on re-reading it, on "re-creating" his novel and himself, as he was fond of saying?

Before moving to a discussion of the specific text *Cómo se hace una novela,* which I shall take the liberty of referring to hereafter as *The Making of a Novel*, perhaps the most important work produced by Unamuno during his six-year exile from 1924 through 1930, the result of the actions of mediocre tyrants, I shall first review Unamuno's evolution as reader and his more important achievements in the phenomenology of reading prior to his exile. Next, I shall proceed to a more detailed examination of *The Making of a Novel* as this relates both to Unamuno's exile and to its meaning with respect to the novel as consciousness.

The early Unamuno, whose literary career begins to evolve toward 1890, and whose first phase culminates in 1897 with the publication of *Peace in War*, a first novel, the scrupulously-researched socio-historical work of a young realist, was a social determinist for whom Hippolyte Taine was a maximal paradigm, in 1890 referred to by Unamuno as "a French colossus whose work is among the greatest, the most profound ever written." This was the Unamuno, who, two years later, pronounced that socialism was "a sacred movement . . . a redemption which would do away with petit military men, insane emperors, and ostentatious erudites," among other things.

Toward 1898, the year following the publication of *Peace in War*, a second Unamuno begins to evolve, the better-known Unamuno, in whose works the eulogies addressed to naturalism, to Taine, to socialism, undergo a racial metamorphosis in the form of anti-naturalistic invective whose ultimate goal seems to have been the justification of new directions in the novel, as well as in the reading of a novel: the French Colossus becomes, for Unamuno, "one of the most dangerous teachers of literary and historical criticism"; the doctrinaire socialists, especially the Marxists, become "intolerant, inflexible fanatics," while the realism of a Zola, to give but one example, is characterized, in Unamuno's words, as "the realism of the toilet."

The first important, concrete literary manifestation of the anti-naturalism of the second Unamuno appears in 1902 with the transitional novella *Love and Pedagogy*, a rather frenetic parody of the rationalism of the times, in which the extrinsic, phenomenal world, as well as its authoritative, impersonal author, are radically reduced, together with the logically-drawn character, displaced by the "indefinition" of abnormal souls and their interior monologue, a first step forward in compelling their reader to collaborate in the so-called "concretization" or "realization" of an equivocal, blurred, enigmatic consciousness. Thus, *Love and Pedagogy* stands as an initial, partial effort toward the more dramatic, obsessive effort which would eventually preoccupy Unamuno over an extended period of some three and a half decades: the effort to invite his reader to participate in the substantiation of his novels by becoming a co-creator, what he was to refer to persistently as the ideal reader, the co-author, or co-poet who accepts the responsibility of restructuring the consciousness of the schematic, fragmented personalities of his novels, as well as the responsibility of restructuring the consciousness of their displaced author.

This extended journey into the phenomenology of reading was to culminate in 1933, with the publication of *The Novel of Don Sandalio, Chess Player*, more than a novel, a complex narration on the ideal reading of a novel and its author, a narration described by Unamuno in his epilogue to *Don Sandalio* as "the novel of my novel," written for readers, he adds, "whom I have created, just as they have created me . . . readers who do not seek the coherent world of the so-called realists."

Excluding the very significant, although brief, 1920 prologue to the *Three Exemplary Novels*, which I cannot discuss here because of time restrictions, the two most important works related to reading published by Unamuno between his 1902 *Love and Pedagogy* and his exile in 1924, are *The Life of Don Quixote and Sancho* (1905)—significantly subtitled in its first edition *According to Miguel de Cervantes Saavedra, Explicated and Commented by Miguel de Unamuno*—and the ontological companion to this impressionistic piece of disruptive, misunderstood criticism, the novel *Mist* (1914). An overview of these two related works, from the point of view of reading theory, follows:

While Unamuno was composing his *Life of Don Quixote* in the summer of 1904, he wrote to one Pedro de Mugica:

> I am writing a *Life of Don Quixote and Sancho According to Miguel de Cervantes, Explained and Commented by Miguel de Unamuno*; these are free meditations on the text, and I include therein whatever I see in it, without caring whether Cervantes willed these inclusions or not. I haven't read a biography of Cervantes and know nothing about his life, nor does it interest me. I consider the *Quixote* an eternal work, authorless, and divorced from the period in which it might have been written.

Notwithstanding the fact that such statements were, and still are, used for the express purpose of denigrating Unamuno, what did all this really mean? What Unamuno's letter *did* mean, regardless of the malice of some of his subsequent critics, was that he was preparing to demonstrate that a book—any book, but especially a great novel—once it is made public, is no longer the exclusive property of a supreme, omnipotent authority whose dictates were formulated for their passive consumption by a passive reader. Above all, it meant that Spain, and its pious Cervantists—all readers, for that matter—were in dire need of radical new directions in criticism, directions which might finally do away with the myopic culling of minutiae from a book and from the life of its imperious, abstracted author, in the name of literary criticism. Additionally, it meant that Unamuno was prepared to demonstrate, through typical hyperbole and apparent irreverance—it is a fact that he really idolized Cervantes—that once conceived, the embryo called a novel can only fully mature, can only be fully completed, by its subsequent appropriation by the multiple hands and consciousness of its future readers; by its synchronic "re-creation" in vital human terms; by its success, or failure, to complement, reinforce, or satisfy the anticipations, expectations, etc., of its multiple and diverse authors throughout history: in brief, by its judgement within a "horizon of expectations," to borrow a recently-coined phrase. That Unamuno forced the reader of his *Don Quixote and Sancho* to meditate on his own novel, on the meaning of the reader's own life and death, is a matter of critical record, impossible to document within the limited scope of this paper.

Mist (1914) should be read as a companion piece to the *Life of Don Quixote and Sancho*, for it is the concrete novelization of all the speculative drama underlying the critical brilliance of 1905, as well as being a maximal example of a character in search of an author, in search of the perspicacious reader who might structure, or restructure, both an amorphous protagonist and his real, amorphous author, Miguel de Unamuno, who dislocates himself as authentic author of *Mist* to the extent even that he becomes a character in his own novel, engaging his protagonist, or "agonist," as Unamuno dubbed him, in a hermeneutic debate whose focus is the autonomous character, the autonomous reader, and the autonomous novel, in the context of the forging of the novel *Mist*, as well as in the context of the forging of a novel known as life and death. In the prologue to the third edition of *Mist*, composed in 1935, Unamuno states that during the twenty-one year interim following the first edition of his novel, *Mist* had become the effort of multiple hands, and that as a result of a preparatory reading for a new prologue, the author himself, Unamuno, had "relived" his own novel. He implies that he has become yet another reader-author of his own book, and refers to the equivocal aspect of *Mist* and to its "collaborators, co-authors, and co-creators" as ideal readers whose ability to immerse themselves in a novel is rewarded by the readers' realization that characters of fiction are valid, real mirrors of the individual readers who contribute to the corporeality of these characters. Fictional characters can be just as real as, or more real than, historical characters long deceased. Since this is so, an author's claim to exclusive rights to his work and creatures is not a valid claim. In the prologue in question, Unamuno also writes that "the Don Quixotes and Sanchos alive in eternity . . . do not belong exclusively to Cervantes . . . each reader makes them relive." So much for Unamuno as receptionist prior to his painful exile, during which, among other works, he composed *The Making of a Novel* in France in 1926 and 1927.

Plagued by the dull skies of Paris, as well as by thoughts of the injustice of his exile, isolated from his family and his culture, unable to concentrate sufficiently in order to read and write, squandering huge blocks of time in unique dialogue with the ceiling in a humble room stacked with partially-read books, lacking the will even to keep himself in clean clothing, a thoroughly dejected Unamuno is finally tempted by the relief of suicide. Nonetheless, the distraught, quixotic genius eventually collects himself and begins to perceive the composition of *The Making of a Novel* as a possible road to salvation—a salvation dependent on concretizing his own exile, his own life, his own novel—in the form of writing, the only salvation possible, really, for a Miguel de Unamuno.

This may be an appropriate juncture to pause and stress that the foregoing synopsis, a prescription for personal salvation, by no means is meant to imply the narcissism or solipsism which Unamuno has too often been accused of, for, in the parafictional commentary with which he consistently interrupts his main narrative in *The Making of a Novel* a narrative on one Jugo de la Raza, who is Unamuno himself Unamuno makes it abundantly clear that his perception of the novel is far removed from its perception as an isolated object of beauty, or of self-indulgence, written either by a disengaged esthete or by a self-indulgent egomaniac exlusively possessed by self-perpetuation. A novel is, rather, for the eminently humanist Unamuno, primarily the social or political statement of an engaged personality. It is social and political to the extent that it is indeed personal, or autobiographical, even as this autobiography is not apparent. For it is a fact, according to Unamuno, that works of fiction which have survived the test of time are all autobiographical, and this would include even Flaubert's *Madame Bovary*, supposedly the most impersonal of all the great nineteenth century novels, or autobiographies. To extrapolate further from Unamuno's suggestive parafiction, the individual novelist concerned with the perpetuation of the self, is really one of the most genuine members of the human community at large, especially of the reading community which reads a novel as it reads the self, since the very personal novelist contributes substantially to the formation of said community.

In its broader dimension, we can reasonably define *The Making of a Novel* as what Unamuno often called a "viviparous" book, an ageneric book, an improvised, extensive hermeneutic circle which contains within it smaller circles of meditation, most of which are primarily addressed to the reader-participant predisposed to immersing himself into these ostensibly grim, frequently vituperous, disjointed circles, so as to finally, having assisted in the completion of Unamuno's work, extricate himself as a more complete, human reader, conscious of his own being and of the enormous social importance of the challenging circles which had forced him to read the author's consciousness of his novel, as well as the writing and re-reading of his novel, as a matter of life and death.

We are now prepared, perhaps, to accept, in deference to Unamuno at least, that the maturing embryo of sixty years ago called *The Making of a Novel* yet awaits its further development by contemporary co-authors, still awaits a synthetic statement which would close the many gaps or so-called "indeterminacies" which apparently, yet only apparently, separate Unamuno's circular esthetic from his intercalated politics. How might we close these gaps and thus complete Unamuno's work?

One way we might do so is to isolate its principally-recurring theme, what we might call its "coordinating axis,"to borrow from modern semiology, and to define this coordinate as the ontological perception of a novel as consciousness. Next, we might define its secondary coordinate as the writer's consciousness of man as political creature, and then relate the two by extrapolating as follows: A novel is truly worthwhile to the extent that it allows for its extrapropriation by the minds of the multiple readers who will continue to complete it throughout its lifetime, and, whether or not it is apparent in its politics, is all the more worthwhile to the extent that the minds which have grasped it are affected in a supremely political, social, human way.

Please allow me to conclude these remarks with a somewhat lengthy quote from the final section of *The Making of a Novel*:

> And I would like to tell you, reader, how a novel is made: how you make a novel, and how you yourself must make your novel. When the inward man, the intra-man, becomes a reader, a contemplator, he must make himself, if he is among the truly

> alert, a reader and contemplator of the character he is making and creating as he reads. He must, in short, be a contemplator, a meditator of his own works. When the inward man, the intra-man . . . transforms himself into a reader, he also makes himself author, that is, actor: When he reads a novel he becomes a novelist, when he reads history, a historian. And every reader who is an inward human being is author of what he reads and is now reading. What you are reading at this moment, reader, on this page, is something you are saying to yourself, and it is as much yours as it is mine.

And I can only hope, kind listeners, that what you have just listened to is as much yours as it is mine. Thank you for your attention.

JUAN RAMON JIMENEZ EN EL EXILIO: NOSTALGIA, ETICA Y OBRA (1939-1948)

José María Naharro-Calderón
University of Maryland

Juan Ramón Jiménez salió de España en 1936 a principios de la guerra civil. Como embajador de buena voluntad y difusor de la causa republicana, el poeta de Moguer desarrolló una labor de incondicional apoyo a la República, en Estados Unidos, Puerto Rico y Cuba. Al final de la guerra, Juan Ramón se unió al grupo de intelectuales que permanecieron exiliados durante la dictadura franquista. En todo el período del exilio donde la muerte lo encontró en 1958, Juan Ramón resistió y rechazó todo intento de exaltación personal o de mejora de sus condiciones geográficas de exiliado por libre elección. Pero son de reciente divulgación los testimonios en los que se percibe sus penalidades de desterrado por partida triple: problemas en torno al alejamiento de su patria, de su obra y a la difusión de ésta.[1]

Una serie de autógrafos hallados en la correspondencia entre su mujer, Zenobia Camprubí y Juan Guerrero Ruiz,[2] el fiel Consul General de la Poesía, muestran la incurable nostalgia juanramoniana a lo largo de los primeros años del destierro. Poco antes de finalizar la guerra, el 14 de febrero de 1939, tras aprender la muerte del hijo menor de los Guerrero, Julio, el poeta da rienda suelta a su elegíaca tristeza, cuando se lamenta con herida sensibilidad, ante la destrucción que rodea a España. Impotente exclama:

> ¡Qué sofocante tristeza diaria! Y Uds. saben que están a cada instante y con cualquier motivo con nosotros, nosotros con ustedes. Es inconcebible, que haya mano que siga con esta venganza, este crimen, este espanto. ¿Y qué podemos hacer dentro y qué fuera de esta España? ¡Malditos los que nos asesinan cínicamente lo mejor de nuestros corazones! ¿Cómo será posible darnos la mano, la mano limpia y la mano

> miserable? He perdido la serenidad y me paso el día gritando. Y mientras tanto, se fueron Juanito Ramón, Julito . . . para siempre. Les abrazo otra vez con desesperación y frío. Juan Ramón.[3]

Con diferentes grados de emoción, estos recuerdos, a veces paralizantes para el poeta, se siguen dando durante los años que nos ocupan en autógrafos al calce de las cartas de Zenobia a Juan Guerrero Ruiz. Unas veces aportan pruebas de la nostalgia a flor de piel; otras, de la imposibilidad del trabajo, al faltarle la obra retenida y saqueada en Madrid.

> (1941) Ya no sé si soy ni de dónde. El tiempo se va y yo paso. ¿En qué terminará todo esto? He perdido toda la ilusión.
> No es posible la resignación, queridos amigos. ¿De dónde? Siempre pensando y hablando de Uds. (de todos Uds. España) y sin posible alegría ya nunca.
> (1942) Cada día más triste y más perdido.
> (1943) ¡Qué daría yo ahora por estar con Uds. (y con mis papeles, mis libros, todo mi trabajo de España!) En cuanto me pongo a trabajar, todo se me queda a medias. ¿Perdido, *eso* para siempre?
> (1946) Siempre pensando en Uds. y en otros de España. ¡Cuánto tiempo pasado!

En un par de cartas de 1942, muestra Juan Ramón una preocupación especial por los sueños. Este repentino interés se ve ratificado por el hecho de que el poema en prosa "Tiempo" empieza y termina con referencias a los sueños:

> Washington se parece tanto a Madrid, ahora en otoño que su belleza me duele materialmente. Prefiero casi no pensar. Dormir es lo mejor. Pero se sueña lo que se piensa.[4] No hay remedio. Escapar solo.

Y en otra, parece sublimar por el sueño la imposibilidad del retorno a España:

> Estoy pasando con el otoño hermosísimo una *terrible época*. Inutilizado por la nostalgia inmensa, para el trabajo y para todo. No sé por qué puerta huir ni hacia dónde.
> Soñé que estaba muerto en Washington, y que, muerto, soñaba que resucitaba en España, y que no podía.

Por esta misma época, Juan Ramón reflexiona en diversos escritos sobre la condición de su lengua, y siente a través de la pérdida de los significantes la mordedura y el aislamiento del exilio. Aunque el ideal lingüístico del poeta se ajuste a la porosidad cultural que produjo en los exiliados el continente americano, pues el español utópico de Jiménez es el conjunto del habla de "todos los españoles [y] todos los hispanoamericanos" que afecta al sistema de la lengua, no deja de advertir el estancamiento de la evolución de su habla materna y la crisis de identidad que le produce.[5]

> Como el idioma es un organismo libre, y vive, muere y se transforma constantemente, el español que se venga hablando en España, desde el año 36, en que yo la dejé, habrá cambiado en doce años, tendrá doce años más o doce menos, según y conforme.
>
> Si yo fuese a España ahora, seguramente hablaría, oiría y hablaría, con duda primero y, luego, un español diferente del que estoy hablando. ¡Yo estraño o el español estraño! [. . .] En todo caso, mi español se ha detenido, hace doce años, en mí. Yo supongo, no lo sé ya tampoco, que hablo como hace doce años. Desconfío de mí ahora y desconfío ahora de lo que leo ahora escrito en España y fuera de España.
>
> Y si quiero recordar, pensar, criticar el español, los españoles, ya no sé lo que leo, lo que hablo ni lo que escribo.[6]

Esta preocupación típica de los poetas del exilio, esa duda ante la supervivencia poética, la retomaba Juan Ramón cuando en un manuscrito inédito titulado "Respuesta concisa",[7] comentaba la obra de Luis Cernuda y al referirse a la personalidad poética del poeta sevillano decía:

> Y usted la consiguió más diferente que otros por (¿su alusión como ve?) hecho de ser usted hijo de madre francesa[8] le ha [ ] una lengua que casi siempre parece una traducción. [. . .] Y es claro, cuando más esté en el estranjero, peor será para usted. A todos nos coje por la lengua el destierro.[9] Pero sobre todo a los que tenían ya la lengua cojida desde niños.

No será hasta su viaje a la Argentina y su posterior instalación en Puerto Rico, cuando Juan Ramón consiga superar el exilio lingüístico y recuperar ese significante divino, suma y división de todos ellos donde se sitúa el sujeto cerológico diseminado de *Animal de fondo*.[10]

> No soy ahora un deslenguado ni un desterrado, sino un consterrado, y por ese volver a lenguarse, he encontrado a Dios en la conciencia de lo bello, lo que hubiera sido imposible no oyendo hablar en mi español. En la casa de Dios estoy ahora

> hablando y España está, en Dios, conmigo. Ahora soy feliz, madre mía, España, madre España, hablando y escribiendo como cuando estaba en tu regazo y en tu pecho.[11]

La vuelta física a España nunca llegó a ser una posibilidad real para Juan Ramón. En una carta de 1939, ante la sugerencia de Juan Guerrero de que retornasen a la península, Zenobia explicaba los motivos, aparentemente no políticos, que les inspiraban el permanecer en América. Desinteresadamente, el matrimonio esperaba ayudar a los amigos de España de la misma forma que lo habían hecho durante la guerra, es decir, desde fuera, además de que las condiciones materiales no sugerían dicho traslado:

> Guerrero, yo creo lo mismo que Ud., que hay que ayudar a España con todas sus fuerzas para que vuelva al vigor suyo y que sólo ha perdido temporalmente desangrada en una guerra que gracias a Dios la ha dejado convalesciendo, no moribunda como pudo haber quedado. Pero creo que la podemos ayudar mucho más desde aquí donde podemos valernos que volviéndonos a encontrar todo lo nuestro deshecho y robado. Yo creo que lo mejor que podría yo llevar a España sería mi corazón sin odios de ninguna clase, pero poco le iba a servir a España si a los dos días de llegar me iba a encontrar con tal cantidad de problemas económicos que en lugar de ayudar a los demás iba a ser carga para los otros. Y todavía esto no es lo peor, sino que Juan que apenas puede ir trampeando con todos los cuidados y una dieta especial, allá sin los alimentos especiales y el frío de Madrid no puede resistir. Es una locura meterse voluntariamente en un atolladero cuando aquí en La Florida puedo cuidar a Juan y además mandar cuanto él quiere a España, pues como somos los dos de gustos sencillos, con lo mío nos basta para vivir como vivimos, sin servicio.[12]

Al poeta le inspiraría poca confianza un país donde su casa era saqueada por los vencedores, sus amigos perseguidos y sus libros prohibidos a la espera de su postura política y geográfica. Una carta de Guerrero del 22 de marzo de 1940, así parece indicarlo:

> En cuanto a las obras de J.R.J. sólo está suspendida su venta "temporalmente" hasta conocerse su actitud, propósito de reintegrarse a España, etc. . . sin que tampoco en esta oficina [de la censura] haya otra cosa, que la firma de aquel primer Manifiesto de julio de 1936, obtenido por la coacción del

> ambiente, y varios de cuyos firmantes están ya en Madrid, depurados favorablemente, por lo cual no se puede considerar como cargo grave.[13]

La actuación de Juan Ramón durante el conflicto civil desmienten categóricamente la opinión de Guerrero sobre las razones que llevaron al poeta a firmar el "Manifiesto" de adhesión a la causa republicana en 1936.[14] Y en "Tiempo" su opinión sobre la muerte de Julián Besteiro, muestran la solidaridad del poeta con la causa republicana: "Qué bello el heroísmo del hombre cultivado y sereno, qué feo el feo heroísmo del hombre bruto y revuelto. Bruto revuelto que deja morir de cárcel a Julián Besteiro, el ecuánime, que caza al hombre honrado y sensitivo que se refujia por necesidad en otro país y lo ahorca o lo fusila, como los dictadores de España [. . .] Aquí tenéis, casticistas, la tan cacareada 'reciedumbre' de España; Azaña, muerto de tristeza, Besteiro de ingratitud, Rivas de venganza [Cipriano Rivas Cherif, sic], en nombre de lo castizo."[15]

En cuanto a los intentos del interior de recuperar a Juan Ramón, también los evitó el poeta en lo posible, siempre que tuvo conocimiento y voto en el asunto, aunque fuera víctima de varias ediciones fraudulentas y tergiversaciones.[16] Uno de los asuntos más interesantes a este respecto, es del tercer nombramiento en 1946 a la Academia, pues como se verá, la carta de rechazo del poeta deja quizá en entredicho su verdadera motivación.[17]

A raíz de las gestiones que Juan Guerrero hacía junto a José Ma. Pemán, director entonces de la Academia, sobre los enseres saqueados del piso madrileño de los Jiménez en la calle de Padilla, éste le pide que gestione con Juan Ramón su ingreso.[18] En carta del 20 de enero de 1946, Juan Guerrero dice:

> Empezaré por una entrevista que sostuve con José Ma. Pemán en el Ministerio de Educación donde me había citado para rogarme le comunicase que un grupo de académicos de la española al que pertenece, deseaban proponer el nombre de J.R. para una de las actuales vacantes; reconociendo su gran valía desean rendirle este homenaje sin que el interesado tenga que hacer otra cosa que aceptarlo ni siquiera tomar posesión si no quiere, y mucho menos que hacer manifestación de otro tipo que no se le pide. Si no pone dificultades sería nombrado próximamente, pues en las esferas oficiales no existe ningún inconveniente para ello.

La alusión de Guerrero a la total exoneración de obligaciones políticas, muestra las necesidades que tenía aquel régimen estrangulado culturalmente de ganar una baza a la España del exilio. Juan Ramón, a mayor distancia de los acontecimientos históricos, se retracta en su contestación a Pemán de algunas de las declaraciones hechas durante los años de la guerra. Sin alterar sus sentimientos pro-republicanos, como lo prueban otros documentos y declaraciones, afirma su ética individualista antidemagógica de raíz krausista ante la marejada política que zarandeaba al buque exiliado:

> Y si escribí yo mismo algunas declaraciones, que en el momento de escribirlas eran exactas, personas y cosas han cambiado tanto, o se han manifestado de modo tan diferente, que no podría volver a decir sino muy poco de lo poco que dije. Porque la cuestión es que yo sigo siendo yo mismo, antidemagogo, como anti otras cosas, por naturaleza y gracia. Mi norma es siempre la misma: primero, la calidad de la persona; que sobre este firme, en todas las ideas puede entenderse con otra persona decente.[19]

La decisión de rechazar el sillón de la Academia carecía por lo tanto de contenido político y venía predispuesta por una vieja actitud antipública de Juan Ramón, lo cual, de cara a la historia, implica de todas formas que el poeta no se prestó a una manipulación que, de haber aceptado el nombramiento, se hubiera producido con toda certeza. En la misma carta a Pemán, señala Juan Ramón que tampoco existieron motivaciones políticas en su negativa a la distribución en España del libro sobre su obra de Carlo Bo, lo cual ratifica su intento en el exilio de presentarse públicamente a distancia de su antigua obra.[20]

Juan Guerrero había quedado al frente de la Embajada española del exilio poético de posguerra. Entre sus múltiples funciones, Guerrero cuidó con esmero de amigo, bibliófilo, poeta, editor y enamorado de la poesía, la obra y la difusión de la obra de Juan Ramón. En 1942, ante el miedo de que aparecieran ediciones piratas de Juan Ramón, caso muy frecuente, y ya que las ediciones extranjeras de los libros del poeta, entre ellas las de Losada argentina, no tenían acceso a la península, Guerrero ideó publicar en la editorial que estaba montando, *Platero y yo*, una edición de Tagore con las versiones de Juan Ramón y Zenobia, así como traducir el primer libro de crítica sobre la poesía de Juan Ramón, por recomendación de José Manuel Blecua.[21] Sin embargo, el 25 de mayo de 1943, Guerrero recibe un cable de Juan Ramón, por el que se le prohibe que edite *Platero y yo*. Con el libro ya compuesto y corregido en la imprenta de S. Aguirre, y repitiendo la mala fortuna de otro intento en 1936, Guerrero declara a Juan Ramón que suspende todo proyecto editorial, excepto el de Carlo Bo.

> Nada de este autor será publicado al menos por Ed. Hispánica, si se exceptúa un corto número de poemas agregados a la traducción española del ensayo crítico de Carlo Bo por estar ya impreso [. . .] Nada más lejos de mi ánimo que causar perjuicio alguno, cuando ha sido mi deseo evitarlo y para ello he trabajado intensamente por espacio de varios meses.

Pocos meses después, Guerrero recibe el 16 de septiembre otro cable de Juan Ramón prohibiéndole la distribución del libro de Carlo Bo. Sorprendido, Guerrero contesta en la del 22 de septiembre lo siguiente:

> Cuando expuse a Uds. el peligro que existía de que apareciesen ediciones fraudulentas de sus traducciones y antologías de su obra, Uds. me escribieron de la siguiente forma: "Society Hill S[outh] C[arolina] 7 de agosto 1942. En este mismo correo va una carta nuestra para Buenos Aires advirtiéndoles que nosotros le damos a Ud. plena autorización para obrar como Ud. entienda más conveniente, sólo pendiente del cablegrama o carta aérea que ellos envíen con su confirmación o reparo. Muchas gracias por ocuparse siempre de nuestras cosas como Ud. lo hace. Z. y J.R.J."

Debido a las dificultades del correo—las cartas de Losada tardaron— y a la errónea creencia de Guerrero de que los libros argentinos no tendrían acceso a España,[22] así como a la ya histórica costumbre juanramoniana de los años treinta, de verse envuelto en una controversia a raíz de alguna publicación antológica, se produjo en la España del interior una polémica en torno a la publicación de una selección de su obra en el libro de Bo, muy similar a la de las antologías mexicanas, (Xavier Villaurrutia et al. y la de Juan José Domenchina).[23] Sorprendido y abatido por esta nueva prohibición, Juan Guerrero trataba de explicar de nuevo sus motivaciones. En una carta del 1 de noviembre, indicaba veladamente que la distancia y diferencias ideológicas parecían motivar aquella decisión:

> Respecto a la traducción del ensayo italiano poco puedo añadir a lo que ya he escrito sobre este asunto. En cuanto a la antología, no creí pudiera perjudicar al autor como añade Ed. Losada, a quien ofrecí el pago de 2000 ptas. por los derechos de inserción de 27 composiciones. Mas bien entendida, era ventajosa la difusión de este libro como propaganda para la venta futura de

> las obras del poeta. Respecto al prólogo, que habiendo sido su autor una de las personas con más nobleza [José María Alfaro] ha mantenido una actitud favorable hacia el autor estudiado, me parecía digno de esta consideración; quizá esto no sea lo mismo estando fuera de España, en el ambiente de 1943. Naturalmente que el tiempo y la distancia hacen variar mucho el aspecto de las cosas y mi equivocación vista a otra luz puede parecer mayor que la realidad.[24]

Una carta de Zenobia a Juan Guerrero, del 29 de agosto de 1943, parece aclarar que Juan Ramón buscaba por aquellos años evitar la inserción en países de habla hispana de su obra publicada antes del exilio, ya que se encontraba en una fase de renovación y había entrado ya en su tercera época, la cual le interesaba dar a conocer y desgajar de su obra anterior.

> J.R. está muy contento con la traducción del libro de Bo aunque consideraba innecesaria la colección de sus poemas: cosa que estaría muy bien en cualquier país extranjero pero injustificada en España, donde se conocen sus poemas. Es decir que el libro de Bo debe considerarse en España como un libro de crítica no como un prólogo para una colección de poesías.

Las declaraciones de Zenobia parecen por lo tanto justificar que Juan Ramón obraba así, como se pudiera extender también al caso de *Laurel* y de la antología de Domenchina, por motivos estrictamente literarios. Ya he apuntado en otro lugar que dicha inhibición me parece ser el deseo de Jiménez de apartarse de las antologías para de esa forma no figurar como poeta canonizado y fosilizado, en un momento de plena creatividad y renacimiento poético. La renovación poética de "Espacio" o *Animal de fondo* mostrarían con efectividad la vitalidad poética de un Juan Ramón, poeta precursor siempre a la cabeza de la modernidad.[25] De ahí que cobre nueva luz lo que le declaraba a José Bergamín, en la segunda carta sin enviar de su polémica con el autor de "El cohete y la estrella:"

> Esta decisión no va sólo con esa casa, es jeneral y ya antigua, como ustedes saben bien. El año pasado negué a otras dos, una europea y otra sudamericana, mi autorización; y si no lo hice en el caso de la anunciada antolojía de otra editorial de Méjico, que no ha llegado a publicarse, fue porque circunstancias personales que nada tienen que ver con lo literario, me movieron a ello [la de Domenchina]; aunque con mi súplica de un cambio mío de lugar, 'un orden cronolójico,' que he considerado siempre

> obligatorio en toda antolojía, ya que lo que cada uno signifique o no, lo significa o no en el sitio en que esté. [. . .] Ustedes saben bien también que mi decisión no es egoísmo poético ni, sobre todo, por aspectos comerciales; que obedece a deseo de apartamiento por confusiones ya antiguas, agravadas día tras día con la mala fe de algunos.[26]

Mientras tanto, el guardián del tesoro juanramoniano quedaba gravemente perjudicado por las dificultades postales y las indecisiones del poeta. Pero tras la recepción de la primera antología de José Manuel Blecua[27] y de otros flamantes títulos de la Hispánica, Juan Ramón decidía reparar el malentendido y darle a la editorial de Guerrero, *Lírica de una Atlántida*, el libro más genuino del exilio juanramoniano, que otros imponderables impidieron que se viera publicado.

Por lo tanto, estos años del exilio trajeron a Juan Ramón, entre otras cosas, un rosario de paradojas: nostalgia de la lengua, de la obra "perdida" en Madrid y de la tierra nativa, pero afirmación de los principios individuales de libertad que le impedían el retorno, a pesar del daño e insatisfacción estética que representaba la separación física con la antigua obra; rechazo del reconocimiento oficial del interior pero enfriamiento político hacia el exilio debido a la desunión del campo transterrado; y finalmente, desagrado ante la reedición de la vieja obra, tanto en el exilio como en el interior, frente a la prolijidad creativa de la tercera época. En contraste con la falsa imagen de un Juan Ramón Jiménez, presentado tantas veces como ajeno al mundanal ruido y preso de sus caprichos, se ve que el poeta mantuvo en aquellos años, a pesar de las contradicciones que le acarreaba su insatisfacción vital, una línea de coherencia. Concilió por lo tanto la esquizofrenia general que le debía producir su condición de exiliado por libre elección, en consonancia con su ética estética ideal de "una armonía de esterior e interior."

Notas

[1] Ver por ejemplo "Desterrado: (Diario poético,)" en Juan Ramón Jiménez, *Guerra en España* (Barcelona: Seix Barral, 1985), págs. 29-65 y en particular mi reseña a este libro en *Hispanic Review* 55 (1987), págs. 121-23. Ver también *Tiempo y Espacio*, ed. Arturo del Villar (Madrid: Edaf, 1986), y el prólogo de Francisco Giner de los Ríos a Juan Ramón Jiménez, *Olvidos de Granada* (Madrid: Caballo Griego para la poesía, 1979), págs. 16-18.

[2] Manuscritos que se conservan en la *Sala Zenobia y Juan Ramón Jiménez* de la Universidad de Puerto Rico bajo el esmerado cuidado de su directora Raquel

Sárraga y colaboradoras, cuya asistencia en mis investigaciones ha sido siempre de incalculable valor. Quiero agradecer a don José Luis Guerrero Aroca y a don Francisco Hernández-Pinzón Jiménez la amable generosidad que me permite divulgar esta correspondencia. Transcribo los fragmentos de las cartas manuscritas sin retocar excepto para algún error ortográfico. En las cartas y manuscritos indico siempre entre corchetes los datos aclaratorios a errores u omisiones, así como los fragmentos no citados, [] y entre manecillas con interrogación (?) aquellos datos dudosos o no aclarados. Alusiones a estos autógrafos de Juan Ramón Jiménez aparecieron en Francisco Javier Díez de Revenga, "Juan Ramón y Juan Guerrero Ruiz: (Algunos datos inéditos)," *Actas del Congreso Internacional de Juan Ramón Jiménez,* 2 vols. (Huelva: Instituto de estudios onubenses, 1983), 1, págs. 287-297.

[3] Juanito Ramón era el ahijado del poeta. Juan Ramón Jiménez Bayo había muerto combatiendo en el bando insurgente. Ver *Guerra en España,* págs. 196-202.

[4] En "Tiempo," pág. 57 dice: "Luego, la traducción de esos estados de vía libre superior o inferior en la que sólo cuenta el entendimiento y la memoria sobre el letargo de la voluntad, suele ser lo más corriente y moliente de lo cotidiano."

[5] Guillermo de Torre en *La aventura y el orden* (Buenos Aires: Losada, 1943), pág. 322 decía que "el exilio habrá prestado a los escritores españoles un beneficio incalculable, una experiencia vital y espiritual del mayor alcance, que de otra suerte pocos habrían resuelto afrontar: el conocimiento y el loor de América."

[6] "El español perdido," *Guerra en España,* pág. 59.

[7] A raíz de la publicación por Luis Cernuda de "Juan Ramón Jiménez," *Bulletin of Spanish Studies* 76 (1942), recogido en *El hijo pródigo* I, 3 (1943), [*Prosa completa* (Barcelona: Barral, 1975), págs. 1341-1367], el poeta de Moguer replicó con su "A Luis Cernuda," *El hijo pródigo* I, 6 (1943) págs. 337-340. Al final de éste añade Juan Ramón la siguiente postdata: "Esto ha sido muy largo, Luis Cernuda; dejo para un segundo artículo puntos de estudio muy convenientes de tocar, puntos de historia, crítica y críticos." [*La corriente infinita: Crítica y evocación* (Madrid: Aguilar, 1961), pág. 179. De igual forma que con muchos de sus proyectos o cartas, Juan Ramón nunca llevó a cabo la idea de editar lo que parece ser uno de los borradores del proyecto [signatura J — 1/141 (21)/144 de la *Sala Zenobia y Juan Ramón Jiménez.*

[8] Exageración de Juan Ramón, ya que la madre de Cernuda había nacido en Sevilla y el origen francés de la rama materna se remontaba al abuelo. La partida de nacimiento de Cernuda dice así: "Que es el hijo del declarante y de su mujer Doña Amparo Bidón y Cuéllar, natural de esta Ciudad [. . .] y por la materna de D. Ulises y Da. Amparo Cuéllar, naturales el primero de Bhediol (Francia), y la segunda de Sevilla, difunta." En José María Capote Benot, *El período sevillano de Luis Cernuda* (Madrid: Gredos, 1971), págs. 147-148.

[9] Preocupación muy similar a la de Jorge Guillén. El poeta de Valladolid decía: "Lo único que he sentido en estos años es que, siendo escritor español, no tenía a mi alrededor la atmósfera de mi lengua. Y he tenido que luchar para no perder vocabulario. Yo lo compensaba con las lecturas en clase, tenía que leer... Pero no estaba uno en el ambiente de su idioma y es siempre fastidioso." Antonio Piedra, "Jorge Guillén: Más allá del soliloquio," *Poesía* 17 (Primavera 1983), pág. 13.

[10] Ver Julia Kristeva, "Poesía y negatividad," *Semiótica*, trad. José Martín Arancibia, 2 vols. (Madrid: Fundamentos, 1978) 2, págs. 55-93, y en particular pág. 89 y ss.

[11] "El milagro español," *Guerra en España*, pág. 284. Círculo lingüístico-vital muy cercano al referido por Cernuda en "la lengua": "—Tras de cruzada la frontera, al oír tu lengua, que tantos años no oías hablada en torno, ¿qué sentiste? —Sentí cómo sin interrupción continuaba mi vida en ella por el mundo exterior, ya que por el interior no había dejado de sonar en mí todos aquellos años [. . .] la lengua del poeta no sólo es materia de su trabajo sino condición misma de su existencia.

Y si la primera palabra que pronunciaron tus labios era española, y española será la última que de ellos salga, determinadas precisa y fatalmente por esas dos palabras, primera y postrera, están todas las de tu poesía. Que la poesía, en definitiva, es la palabra." "Variaciones sobre tema mexicano." *Prosa completa,* pág. 117.

[12] En respuesta a la de Juan Guerrero del 19 de agosto de 1939, en la que sugería el retorno debido al supuesto apoliticismo juanramoniano: "Gracias a Dios no han sido nunca políticos, siempre han trabajado dentro y lejos de su patria, por ella y aun cuando por la circunstancia de su larga estancia en el extranjero, habrán de vencer algunas dificultades para el regreso, todo podrá justificarse, y continuar aquí en paz su vida de glorioso trabajo." Y en la del 30 de abril de 1941, insistía: "Sobre todo, la soledad espiritual que padecemos es muy grande, y yo hubiera pensado ya alguna vez en marcharme con mi cargo anterior a otra parte, si no pensara que esto acabará alguna vez y Uds. volverán entre nosotros. Esta es la mejor esperanza que me mantiene, y la ilusión de que con mi presencia aquí, sirvo de guardián para aquellos originales rescatados que tienen un valor espiritual inmenso, que no se ha sabido estimar por quien debiera valorarlos mejor. Esta esperanza de su regreso se enlaza con la posibilidad de hacerlo. Ya sé bien, que aun cuando no existieran dificultades de otro orden, la guerra europea es causa bastante para no hacer el viaje. Por tanto hasta que concluya, no espero nada. Y en realidad toda la vida española, en todos los órdenes está ligada al resultado final de la contienda. Sobre esto no creo exista duda alguna [. . .] Cuando me pregunta alguien, siempre contesto, que cuando haya paz completa volverán, pues una persona delicada de salud (¡y de sentimientos!) no podría resistir las privaciones que generalmente se padecen y que podrían poner en riesgo su vida." Regreso que el 2 de diciembre de 1945, Zenobia hacía factible

en términos poco comprometidos: "Con la conformidad de Juan Ramón nosotros pensamos siempre ir a España, cuando nuestras circunstancias y de trabajo nos lo permitan, tomando [sic] un pisito pequeño para vivir allí temporadas largas." A lo que Juan Guerrero contestaba esperanzado en su carta del 14 de abril de 1946, dando muestras del inmenso apego que sentía por ambos amigos, pero también augurando que aquel reencuentro, como aseverarían los años, no se realizaría jamás: "Nos alegra lo que dice Zenobia en su carta última sobre su deseo de volver a España. Para mí, perdería gran parte de sentido el resto de mi vida si no volviera a verles, pero comprendo que tiene grandes dificultades organizar su nueva instalación en España. Y quiero confiar en el porvenir, aunque a veces me encuentro viejo y cansado."

[13] En su carta del 30 de abril de 1940 Guerrero insistía que "por esto, su prudente actitud la encuentro justificada y necesaria, ya que hay que procurar que no se le crea unido políticamente con quienes en realidad no tuvo nunca afinidad, ni contacto. Su hondo amor a España está por encima de todas las contingencias por profundas que éstas sean, y juntamente con su obra merecen que cuando la paz haga posible la vuelta tengan abiertas las puertas de la patria con todo honor y garantía del máximo respeto."

[14] Ver *Guerra en España*, págs. 116-119, "Declaraciones del gran Juan Ramón Jiménez," *El Mono Azul*, 1 (1936), pág. 3 y "Palabras de Juan Ramón Jiménez," *Hora de España* 9 (1937), págs. 59-60.

[15] pág. 77.

[16] Ver mi "Censura y recuperación en la España franquista: 'Enredos' en torno al exilio: Antonio Machado y Juan Ramón Jiménez," *Revista monográfica* 1, 2 (1986), de próxima publicación.

[17] Había ya sido propuesto en 1931 y 1934; invitación que Juan Ramón había rechazado de acuerdo con su característica discreción pública y su devoción por la "Obra."

[18] Ver *Guerra en España*, págs. 214-229.

[19] *Cartas literarias*, págs. 95-96. Para el krausismo de Juan Ramón ver Francisco Javier Blasco Pascual, *La poética de Juan Ramón Jiménez: Desarrollo, contexto y sistema* (Salamanca: Studia Philologica Salmanticensia, 1981), págs. 107-118.

[20] "Y no piense usted que yo esté relacionando esto [el rechazo al nombramiento a la Academia] con nada político, como no fue nada político mi prohibición de que circulara un libro reciente sobre mí. Pero Guerrero alude discretamente a este punto y quiero contestar que no, que no se trata de eso." *Cartas literarias*, pág. 95.

[21] Carlo Bo, *La poesía con Juan Ramón* (Florencia: Edizione di Revoluzione,

1941). *La poesía de Juan Ramón Jiménez*, versión española de Isabel de Ambia, prólogo de José María Alfaro, selección de poemas a cargo de Juan Guerrero Ruiz (Madrid; Editorial Hispánica, 1943). Curiosamente, una revista falangista, reseñaba en tono conciliador el libro de Bo y pedía en línea con lo plasmado por la revista *Escorial*, una superación de la escisión ideológica entre exilio e interior, proceso que estudio en varios artículos y un libro de próxima terminación: "Y considerar el volumen que 'Hispánica' traduce como el principio de una labor por efectuar que no sólo en este caso, sino en tantos otros, analice, valore, perfile la personalidad extraordinaria de tanto poeta español que necesitan [sic] para su gloria en el tiempo algo más que enemigos o amigos." *Haz*, 7, (1943), pág. 51. Esta moderación se veía ratificada por otra anterior: "[. . .] Cuando el enemigo escribe mejor que nosotros y no comulga con nuestro ideario o nuestro credo, es noble, necesario e indicado cantar por delante las excelencias de su oficio." "A sonetazo limpio," *Haz*, 69, (1942), pág. 4.

[22] En una carta de Ed. Losada del 23 de julio de 1943 que llegó a manos de Guerrero el 23 de octubre, se le decía: "En el mes de abril último se firmó un convenio de intercambio de libros entre España y la Argentina en el cual consta que desaparecerán absolutamente todas las trabas, gravámenes, etc. . . que puedan entorpecer la entrada de libros españoles en la Argentina y la de libros argentinos en España, y por lo que respecta a la Argentina sí se hace en términos absolutos. La única limitación es la que se refiere a la censura de orden político, es decir que no podrán entrar a España libros que atenten contra su actual sistema de gobierno. El tratado debía de entrar en vigor el mes de su firma, o sea, hacia mediados del mes de mayo."

[23] *Laurel: Antología de la poesía moderna en lengua española* (México: Séneca, 1941). Sobre la muy disputada antología ver, *Guerra en España*, págs. 238-252 y Octavio Paz "Laurel y la poesía moderna," *Quimera* 26 y 27 (1982-1983), págs. 10-19 y 12-22. Juan José Domenchina utilizó profusamente en el prólogo de su *Antología de la poesía española contemporánea (1900-1936)*, epílogo de Enrique Díez Canedo (México: Atlante, 1941) el artículo de Juan Ramón "Crisis del espíritu en la poesía española contemporánea (1899-1936)," *Nosotros* 48-49 (1940), págs. 165-182. Aunque no incluyó poemas del destierro, esta antología fue la primera editada por un exiliado. A Juan Ramón le molestó profundamente el excesivo protagonismo que le daba el figurar a la cabeza de la antología. Para una versión de los incidentes de los años treinta y de *Laurel*, ver Nigel Dennis, *Perfume and Poison: A Study of the Relationship between José Bergamín and Juan Ramón Jiménez* (Kassel: Edition Reichenberger, 1985), págs. 46-79 y 94-112.

[24] Guillermo de Torre en carta del 11 de octubre de 1943 le decía a Juan Guerrero: "Hace dos días hemos recibido un cable del autor de "Platero" desde Washington. En él nos dice que está completamente de acuerdo con esta carta enviada a Ud. y de la cual le hicimos conocer una copia. Nos agrega que está disconforme con la actitud de la Ed. Hispánica terminando textualmente:

'Prohibido la publicación de nada mío. Todo arreglo sometido a Ud.'[. . .] Ello confirma como le decíamos que la publicación ahí de ese autor no favorece a nadie y que, en todo caso, antes de intentar nada nuevo, más prudente es esperar a que las circunstancias del libro en general se normalicen." El fantasma de dicho malentendido seguiría persiguiendo a Guerrero durante varios años. En carta del 30 de abril de 1946, a raíz de la inserción de Juan Ramón Jiménez en una de las tres antologías desautorizadas por el poeta, publicadas en la España del interior en 1946, [Alfonso Moreno, *Poesía española actual* (Madrid: Editora Nacional, 1946), y *Federico Carlos Sáinz de Robles, Historia y antología de la poesía española contemporánea (en lengua castellana): Del siglo X al XX* (Madrid: Aguilar, 1946)] decía: "C. González Ruano ha publicado una voluminosa antología de la poesía española contemporánea desde S. Rueda a los niños de hoy. Yo no he intervenido en nada en este libro, que le envío a título de información aunque me contrarían algunas citas que he visto." *Antología de poetas españoles contemporáneos en lengua castellana* (Barcelona: Gustavo Gili, 1946). En la sección dedicada a Juan Ramón decía G. Ruano lo siguiente: "Una herencia estética baudeleriana en contraposición con Verlaine, de cuya contaminación, como señala muy sagazmente Carlo Bo (*La poesía de Juan Ramón Jiménez*, Madrid, 1943) se salva intentando una vía interior del todo [. . .] Recientemente (Madrid, 1943) se ha publicado *La poesía de Juan Ramón Jiménez*, ensayo de Carlo Bo, cuya edición original fue publicada en Florencia (1941). La traducción se debe a Isabel de Ambía, lleva un prólogo de José Ma. Alfaro, una bibliografía de las obras de Juan Ramón Jiménez y una selección de poemas hecha por Juan Guerrero Ruiz." Págs. 159-160.

[25] Utilizo el término "precursor" siguiendo a Harold Bloom, *The Anxiety of Influence* (New York, Oxford, 1973).

[26] *Guerra en España*, pág. 244. No hubo problemas sin embargo para figurar en la antología de Francisco Giner de los Ríos, *Las cien mejores poesías españolas del destierro* (México: Signo, 1945). Allí aparecían únicamente poemas del exilio.

[27] *Las flores en la poesía española* (Madrid: Hispánica, 1944).

MOTHERS RECOLLECTING DAUGHTERS IN *EL CUENTO DE NUNCA ACABAR*

Andrew Bush
Vassar College

for Sarah Stewart

Each seemed a child, like me, on a loose perch,
Holding to childhood like some termless play.
Hart Crane

Writing about the relation between translations and original works as an issuing forth and a form of survival in "The Task of the Translator," Walter Benjamin urged that "The idea of life and afterlife in works of art should be regarded with an entirely unmetaphorical objectivity" (71). One may read in this light his remarks concerning death in "The Storyteller": "The novel is significant, therefore, not because it presents someone else's fate to us, perhaps didactically, but because this stranger's fate by virtue of the flame which consumes it yields us the warmth which we never draw from our own fate. What draws the reader to the novel is the hope of warming his shivering life with a death he reads about" (101). These poignant words may be clarified with an unmetaphorical objectivity: the death that warms the reader is not that of hero or heroine, who, after all, quite frequently survives the machinations of the plot, but of the text itself. Thus at the closing of each text a reader will experience the labor of mourning as Freud understood it: a love of literature is withdrawn, recuperated and made available for new investment in a subsequent text. Whereas those who return to the same text, repeating it by rereading or rewriting—including Benjamin's translators—would be likewise those who refuse to mourn.

Rereading and retelling, then, would be cases of a peculiar delinquency: a rejection of the labor of mourning in favor of a termless play of repetition. The Freudian verdict is melancholia, truly the uncanny step "beyond the pleasure principle." And it might be noted that in his essay by that title, a peculiar love letter to all who mourn, Freud, therapist for a civilization, seeks precisely to put a term to melancholy, leading it back to the governance of the reality principle. Yet even Freud has his moment of doubt: "If we are to die ourselves, and first to lose in death those who are dearest to us, it is easier to submit to a remorseless law of nature, to the sublime *Ananke* [Necessity], than to a chance which might perhaps have been escaped. It may be, however, that this belief in the eternal necessity of dying is only another of those illusions which we have created 'To bear the burden of existence' " (39). Freud's vision of destiny is inherited from the Romantics, amongst whom it may be found, for instance, chiseled into Hugo's *Notre-Dame de Paris,* where the prefatory note to the 1831 edition begins: "Il y a quelques années qu'en visitant, ou pour mieux dire, en furetant Notre-Dame, l'auteur de ce livre trouva, dans un recoin obscur de l'une des tours ce mot gravé a la main sur le mur: ANANKE" (29, my transcription). Hugo's note closes, "C'est sur ce mot qu'on a fait ce livre" (29)—which might equally be said of *Beyond the Pleasure Principle*—so that *"Ananke",* the text inscribed in stone, becomes itself the cornerstone of the edifice of *Notre-Dame de Paris.* For Hugo, that is, the necessity governing the novel lies not at the close of the text, but before or below, as of course it will for Freud, though the text he studies be the psyche. In Hugo's terms, then, the particular concern of this reconnaissance of Carmen Martín Gaite's *El cuento de nunca acabar* will focus less on the hand that inscribes an all but forgotten text, than on the need to recover a text that is already a memory: a reading *en furetant* that I refer to as *recollecting.*

Otherwise stated, Freud resolves his doubts in the face of a Romantic *Ananke* by reaffirming the dualism of the drives: the sexual drives lead to life and afterlife (in the engendering of offspring), whereas the death-drive, manifest as a compulsion to repeat, bears us to an inevitable death inherent in all organisms. As concerns an author, however, who must die like the rest of us no doubt, but who must lose first in death, that is see through to an end, the texts dearest to her, as in the case of *El cuento de nunca acabar*, further reflection is required. Whereas for Freud our fate is implacable, but lies behind us, here the compulsion to repeat, figured forth as an obligation to recollect, presents that very chance by which the necessity of death might be escaped. For Martín Gaite, the afterlife precedes us—it is our pretext.

The erotic metaphor, even allegory that drives her book to its termination, to a "Ruptura de relaciones" (285-304), must be set in opposition to such a compulsion. For although Martín Gaite will liken the writing of the *El cuento de nunca acabar* to a love affair, initiated in clandestine trysts in hotel rooms, passing through years of tumultuous cohabitation and ending with the break up of a home, the text is rather a daughter than a lover, I would contend, and not without an awareness of the tragic implications for the writer. It is the daughter who informs the writing with her termless play, indeed it is the daughter who will compel recollection in the scene of instruction that marks the conception and baptism of the text.[1] For Martín Gaite learns what mothers must have known since the biblical time of Sarah, even if Freud apparently did not, namely that the characteristic repetition of children's play is first and foremost a denial that any game must come to a natural end. To a child, endings are merely interruptions imposed from without by another will with a greater authority. Hence, *El cuento de nunca acabar* may be read beyond the Freudian dualism as a speculation upon the dialectical opposition of recollection, whose medium is the daughter, and interruption, whose agent is the mother. Caught between the two, mother no less than daughter, Martín Gaite defines the role of the storyteller as a revolutionary struggle, rather than a stable synthesis: the mother enjoining the daughter to desist from the play of textual proliferation; the daughter ever seeking to overcome the limits set by the injunction. The paradigm for narration thus becomes the bed-time story, which is told to put the child to sleep, but which the child demands in order to stay awake always a moment longer.

The narration of the mother-daughter bond, or rather the conception of narration as a relation between mother and daughter, finds theoretical expression in *El cuento de nunca acabar* in the section "Reflexiones en el parque" (105-15). This episode begins as a defense of reading, but is transformed into a scene of writing through the interplay of attraction and distraction. The initial project concerns the means by which the narrator, a mother, may involve her daughter in the play of other children, so that "me dejara leer el libro que traía en el bolso" (107). With this end in view, the mother narrates: "Uno de los experimentos que yo hacía por entonces era el de ponerme muy seria y abstraída a dibujar en la arena espirales y rayitas con un palo, menester al que me entregaba con toda pausa y concentración durante largo rato. Fue un recurso que nunca me falló" (109). By turning her own attention from reading to this writing in the sand, her daughter is distracted, and she and the other children become engaged in a common pursuit: "el incentivo del juego nacido ya los envolvía de forma espontánea, brindándoles sus tres funciones de placer compartido, de ficción y de adivinanza, que—ya cada una por separada, ya en mezcla simultánea—informan como constantes la esencia de cualquier juego que quepa analizar. Y, según he visto luego, la de cualquier narración, como juego por excelencia que es" (111). This meditation reflects upon *El cuento de nunca acabar* itself, which may be identified as just such a game inaugurated by an author who then leaves the text to play among its readers.

The narrator's further remarks serve to divide those children into two categories of readers: incipient literary critics, who guess at the meaning of the lines drawn in the dust, offering their own interpretations, on the one hand, and on the other, nascent narrators in their own right, who take the tracing as a pretext for their own drawing, their own fictions. In either case the immediate consequence is that the children are soon playing together in the dirt. In thus inscribing her text, literally her theoretical ground-work, the narrator sets in motion a displacement, no less literal, of the dust that comes to be imprinted upon the children themselves: textual offspring of her writing.

The flaubertian author would then withdraw, leaving the children to proceed without further invention, and freeing herself to read in peace, were it not that she is in turn distracted, drawn by their dust jackets as it were: "Y yo, que me había retirado de aquel teatro sin que nadie lo notase ni me echara de menos, alzaba de vez en cuando los ojos de mi libro y veía a aquellos diligentes y fingidos jardineros, tenderos o soldados, les oía pactar, discutir, imponerse unos a otros el texto de su propia función improvisada" (112). The dramatic text of the children at play imposes itself on her, no less than on them so that the book that the mother has brought with her is intermittently forgotten. And it is this reengagement of the author by the text of the children, the text that is the children, in short the text that she has brought forth from herself and her recollections of her own childhood that serves as a model for the love between narrator and narration in *El cuento de nunca acabar*, rather than a form of seduction appropriate to a theory of narrative erotics. The storyteller loves her tale as a mother her daughter—daughter and text, translations of herself, drawing her back ceaselessly to her past.

The fundamental pleasure of reading according to this theoretical model lies in the comparison between present observation and "imágenes resucitadas del desván de mi infancia" (107). The scene of writing is itself a reminiscence, whose prior scene of instruction may be mapped onto the "geografía narrativa" (351-52 and 402) of Martín Gaite's textual world with precision. The urban park recalls the *campo* of her childhood; the drawing on the ground tropes upon a prior plowing of the fields. Hence it might be possible to give these "apuntes sobre la narración, el amor y la mentira", the subtitle of the book, a generic designation. *El cuento de nunca acabar* is I propose, a tractate but also a tract, a *tratado*, and as such a reference work for writers and for mothers who are daughters; it might bear a revised subtitle: Martín Gaite's *Georgics*.

The reflexive model for narration diverts any possibility of ending into a recollection of abandoned projects. The text cannot end because it does not know how to begin. At the outset of "Reflexiones en el parque," for example, Martín Gaite declares: "Llegué a divertirme bastante e incluso a tomar notas para una novela que llevaba por título: "El parque", y que luego nunca encontré ocasión para ponerme a escribir" (107). This *novela de nunca empezar* becomes an intercalated tale that reflects the whole of *El cuento de nunca acabar*, which itself has no less difficulty in beginning (witness its seven prologues) than in coming to an end.

Once under way, however, the tracing of the text as a retracing of one's steps "a campo través" (the title of the second section which includes "Reflexiones en el parque") does not die, as Freud would have it, "for *internal* reasons" (Freud's italics, 32). Martín Gaite narrates this ending of the text as a death, but one imposed from outside the boundaries of the game. A mother arises who lacks eyes to read the text of the children's play: "Pero, Pablito, ¿Qué haces ahí?, no juegues con la tierra, ¡como vaya!", is her battle cry, "que no solía ser atendido más que cuando tomaba un tono de autoridad inesquivable y determinaba la formal prohibición, acompañada a veces del desplazamiento de la madre en persona hacia el campo de la sedición rebelde, con la consiguiente baja de uno de los pequeños soldados [. . .]" (113). And the narrator, too, will take on the mother's role, when she announces in "Ruptura de relaciones", "Ya está. Se acabó" (289), only to specify: "Y de repente esta tarde he tenido la revelación fulminante: ¡Basta! Me falta muchísimo, pero basta. No es que lo acabe, es que lo dejo. Lo dejo sin acabar" (293). In either case the interruption bears an arbitrary relation to the play of the text, which is not *acabado* when the accident of ending befalls it.

Yet *El cuento de nunca acabar* exceeds even the promised end. The text will not close with "Ruptura de relaciones," but rather will go on to a fourth chapter, "Río revuelto". Nor will the latter end with its final note, "Re-anudar" (403), which signals instead that "el azar interrumpió" the thread of the tale the very chance that might have been escaped, the very interruption that may be restituted by the process of recollection. In effect, Martín Gaite concludes by *retracting* the possibility of concluding. "Reflexiones en el parque" may be taken as a microcosm of the whole in this respect, for it is in itself a *cuento de nunca acabar*, closing (or rather refusing to close) as a promise to continue: "Acerca de los juegos infantiles aventuré también otras teorías, derivadas de los datos que me proporcionaba el comportamiento de los niños en el parque. Pero no las quiero aglomerar ahora. Por mis cuadernos están. Ya irán saliendo" (115).

Martín Gaite is enabled to continue beyond the stated bounds of her own maternal prohibition, because she is reeducated by her daughter, that is both by the text that she is inscribing and intermittently rereading (the various notebooks that are the sources of these *apuntes*), and by the girl who compels her mother to recollect. Drawing from a file entitled "Frustraciones e incompletos" (295), that is once again a prototype of *El cuento de nunca acabar*, the narrator records a scene of instruction in which the mother's silencing prohibition is overturned by the seditious daughter. *"—Nada, tengo sueño, me voy a dormir ya"* (the entire passage is italicized by the author; 298), declares the mother, cutting off her child's recollections of a day in the country. At the same time she forecloses her own reminiscences, for the daughter had unwittingly become a living memory, reenacting an analogous moment on a more distant day in a more distant countryside in her mother's childhood. Mother and daughter each in turn had imagined an ideal text, "un dibujo completo donde no quedara nada por meter, "también lo que no se ve, ¿sabes?)" (296). The mother interrupts this proliferation of memory upon memory, memory within memory, feeling threatened by the potential for termless play: "Era el vértigo de perder pie como un terror a desprenderse y rodar por los abismos" (298). More concretely she fears that this bed-time story will only prevent her daughter from sleeping. It is the daughter who must finally instruct the mother in the process of *reanudar*. She will oblige the mother to turn back to the origins of their dialogue; she will compel her to recollect: *"—Oye—me dijo de repente—. ¿Por dónde empezamos a hablar esta tarde?"* (299). Called upon to *hacer memoria*, to recollect a first word, the mother will respond in time by initiating the rewriting of the word, the memory and the call as an entry in an unfinished notebook that becomes, in retrospect, a premonition: " . . . no, sería inabarcable, sería el cuento de nunca acabar" (301). The story teller lives on, so the story cannot die.

Notes

[1] An underlying theoretical concern of the present essay, although one which must be referred to only in passing awaiting a more ample elaboration in a different context, is the debate engaged between Bloom's "scene of instruction" and Derrida's "scene of writing". While *El cuento de nunca acabar* practices a deconstructive reading of itself—indeed the whole of the text *is* that deconstructive reading—and in that sense may be aligned with Derrida's work (and Pedro Cuperman's discussion of Cortazar's *Rayuela* here at the Syracuse conference), I would situate Martín Gaite's text, particularly in its understanding of recollection, on Bloom's side of the polemic. Of course Martín Gaite departs radically from Bloom's oedipal poetics by presenting a mother-daughter paradigm, where Bloom speaks insistently in terms of the relation of fathers and sons. I offer this suggestion here in order to place *El cuento de no acabar* in the context of post-structuralist literary study, updating the explicit polemic that Martín Gaite engages with structuralism, which, if more topical at the time of her *apuntes*, was already outdated by the time of publication.

Works Cited

Benjamin, Walter. *Illuminations.* Trans. Harry Zohn. Ed. Hannah-Arendt. New York: Schocken, 1969.

Bloom, Harold. "The Primal Scene of Instruction," in his *A Map of Misreading*. New York: Oxford University Press, 1975: 41-62.

Derrida, Jacques. "Freud et la scene de l'écriture" in his *L'écriture et la différence.* Paris: Seuil, 1967: 293-340.

Freud, Sigmund. *Beyond the Pleasure Principle*. Trans. and Ed. James Strachey. New York: Norton, 1975.

Hugo, Victor. *Notre-Dame de Paris: 1482.* Paris: Garnier-Flammarion, 1967.

Martín Gaite, Carmen. *El cuento de nunca acabar*. Madrid: Trieste, 1983.

LA POESIA DE LUIS RIUS, O LA CONSECUENCIAS DEL EXILIO EN UNA PROMOCION FRONTERIZA

Susan Rivera
University of New Mexico

En su libro *Literatura española del último exilio*,[1] Antonio Ferres y José Ortega distinguen cuatro diferentes grupos entre los españoles exiliados: A) Los que salen inmediatamente después de la Guerra con una obra literaria publicada (Sender, Ayala). B) Los que salen de niños y escriben su obra desde el extranjero, aunque publiquen fuera o dentro de España (Roberto Ruiz, Manuel Durán, Carlos Blanco). C) Escritores que a partir de la década de los cincuenta, residen en el extranjero con obra publicada fuera y dentro de España (Juan Goytisolo, Antonio Ferres, López Pacheco, J.M. Valverde). D) Sería posible señalar además otro apartado donde se incluyen obras que han tenido que publicarse en el extranjero, obras exiliadas escritas por autores que residen en España (López Salinas, José Agustín Goytisolo, Luis Goytisolo, Caballero Bonald). De todos ellos, el grupo formado por los hijos de los republicanos refugiados, que salieron de España en la infancia o primera adolescencia, es el que menos audiencia y atención crítica ha recibido, sobre todo en su país de nacimiento. Entre ellos cabría destacar, por su número y por su coherencia, el grupo de poetas que se estableció y formó concretamente en México. Se trata de una generación que, surgida en los años 50, todavía había tenido un contacto, por mínimo que hubiera sido, con España, y por esta razón representa el último límite de los escritores españoles "transterrados". Entre los principales integrantes de la llamada "segunda generación de poetas hispano-mexicanos" destacan los nombres de Ramón Xirau, Manuel Durán, César Ródríguez Chicharro, Jomi García Ascot, Tomás Segovia, Luis Rius, José Pascual Buxó, Enrique de Rivas, Angelina Muñiz, Federico Patán y Nuria Parés.

La falta de atención por parte de la crítica española o hispanista se debe quizá a la ambigüedad misma que los caracteriza. El hecho de haber nacido en España los hace españoles y, sin embargo, la circunstancia de haber vivido en México desde una edad tan temprana, y haberse educado y formado enteramente en su país "heredado", aunque fuese en un ambiente muy español, ha hecho que la asimilación a la cultura mexicana resultara casi completa. Se encuentran, pues, situados entre dos mundos sin pertenecer plenamente a ninguno. Según Francisco de la Maza es una generación "nepantla" o "a la mitad"; según Luis Rius:

> Era demasiado temprano para que al llegar a México, fuéramos ya, como nuestros padres, españoles; y demasiado tarde para poder ser mexicanos. Somos, pues, seres fronterizos. Definitivamente, no podemos renunciar ni a la españolidad ni a la mexicanidad, que a un mismo tiempo, y por propio derecho, poseemos.[2]

La ambivalencia no termina aquí; algunos críticos han llegado a cuestionar incluso su condición de exiliados, puesto que en su caso el exilio no fue realmente elegido ni exactamente voluntario, sino más bien decidido por otros, "heredado"; como dice Nuria Parés en uno de sus poemas: "Nadie eligió su herencia/ ni tú ni yo. Nosotros no elegimos." Aunque esta falta de elección o de voluntad sea evidente, no parece suficiente para negar su condición de exiliados, especialmente porque ellos mismos se sienten y declaran como tal. Es innegable que el exilio no debe entenderse sólo como la ausencia física de un país sino también (y quizá sobre todo) como una actitud espiritual y personal. Es imprescindible, por lo tanto, comprender la especial significación que la experiencia del exilio cobra en ellos. Paradójicamente y al contrario de lo que podría pensarse, estos niños, ya adultos, sienten quizá todavía más profundamente que sus predecesores el desarraigo propio del destierro, pero de una manera mas ontológica y existencial. A este respecto explica José Ramón Marra-López:

> Si las anteriores generaciones—en mayor o menor grado—poseían vivencias de la tierra perdida, se hallan unidos a ella por su vida pasada, entrañable en la ausencia, este nuevo grupo resulta el más hondamente exiliado de todos, sin encontrarse en parte alguna, ni siquiera en la región de los recuerdos.[3]

Esta dificultad a la hora de clasificarlos de una manera coherente y global no tendría graves repercusiones si no fuera porque la confusión los ha convertido, literalmente, en una especie de "generación perdida". Pertenecen plenamente a la literatura mexicana, pero por circunstancias históricas de las cuales en parte son el producto y casi siempre las víctimas, pertenecen también, con toda justicia, a la literatura española. Su reivindicación es necesaria y urgente para completar el cuadro de la historia de la poesía española contemporánea. Según Angel González:

> . . .si la guerra civil y sus consecuencias acabarían siendo el efecto traumático o la materia de reflexión que configuran, en principio, uno de los denominadores más comunes de la generación española del medio siglo o de "los niños de la guerra", esa promoción no puede darse por completa hasta que en ella se integren los poetas que, dispersos prematuramente por el exilio, escribieron bajo la presión de las mismas circunstancias. Tan de la guerra, o más si cabe, fueron los niños que se vieron obligados a salir de España en 1939 como los que nos vimos forzados a quedarnos.[4]

Del grupo de poetas hispano-mexicanos, Luis Rius es, sin duda, uno de los más importantes por la extraordinaria calidad de su obra, y también uno de los más representativos de las actitudes y reacciones generacionales frente al drama del exilio. Para Luis Rius la poesía obedece a un propósito: salvar lo más íntimo de su ser. Según se deduce al leer sus poemas, lo más íntimo del ser de Luis Rius es un decidido sentimiento de nostalgia y de ausencia. En palabras de Francisco Carrasquer, "En el fondo, la buena pluma se mueve por nostalgia. . . Decir nostalgia es decir ausencia, y ausencia forzada es decir exilio".[5] El exilio es, pues, la raíz de la desolación del poeta, pero lo interesante en este caso es el proceso de transformación del concepto de "exilio", tal como se manifiesta en su obra y en su propio "ser". El origen de la inquietud del poeta se debe a una circunstancia puramente biográfica, el destierro, pero el sentimiento de abandono o de pérdida de un bien concreto—la patria—se profundiza y amplía hasta transcender los límites de la peripecia personal y convertirse en una angustia definitivamente existencial, ontológica. No es ya la pérdida de la patria lo que le aflige sino la inconsistencia del ser, el fundamento oscuro e irracional de la existencia, y así su poesía deriva en un íntimo y angustiado soliloquio, limpio de cualquier contaminación histórica o circunstancial. En la poesía de Luis Rius el "yo" lírico llega a ser imagen de lo universal, exponente de toda la condición humana. No es la suya una desesperanza relacionada con el "aquí y el ahora", sino la desesperanza que advertimos en cualquier parte y siempre.

En uno de sus poemas primerizos, del que su autor prescindirá posteriormente, Luis Rius refleja todavía de una manera explícita la obsesión por la patria perdida, España, y la expone con una retórica y un tono sentimental heredado de los poetas mayores en edad, compatriotas que él conoció en el exilio. Se trata de una composición mimética, que repite motivos y símbolos que configuran lo que Max Aub llamó penetrantemente "una España de segunda mano"; reacción explicable en un poeta muy joven que, al carecer de las vivencias y experiencias directas de la patria perdida a la que cantaba, tenía que apelar al testimonio e incluso a las mismas palabras de aquellos que habían vivido de adultos todo lo que él no recordaba de su infancia. Sin duda, Luis Rius hablaba por boca de León Felipe en versos como los siguientes:

Tuyo soy porque llevo
un bordón en la mano
y un sayal de romero
y voy peregrinando
clamando por justicia
y como tú, España, no la hallo.

Ese levantar la voz "clamando por justicia" delata también el intento de integrarse en el coro, tan numeroso entonces, de los poetas "sociales", intento muy pronto abandonado. Pero aunque casi todo en ese poema—tema, tono, símbolos—es ajeno, hay en él algo que ya separa a Luis Rius de los poetas a los que, como buen aprendiz, imita: la conciencia de que él no conoce lo que añora, no sabe lo que es esa realidad a la que quiere, con todo el terco empeño de su voluntad, pertenecer:

Tuyo soy aunque el tiempo
tu perfil de mi mente haya borrado.
Ni conozco tus mares,
ni conozco tus campos.
Nunca he visto las sendas
que recorrió tu infante don Pelayo;
jamás vi la Valencia
que rindiose al esfuerzo del buen Cid castellano. . .

No tardará el joven poeta en desprenderse de la retórica y las obsesiones heredadas de sus mayores. Es significativo a ese respecto que España, invocada tres veces en el poema citado, sólo aparezca nombrada en dos ocasiones en el volumen que recoge su poesía completa, tal y como su autor la dejó organizada pocos meses antes de su muerte. En uno de esos textos, España se configura como una realidad, aunque siempre entrañable, contemplada en una borrosa y definitiva lejanía:

Compañero, allá lejos,

desde esta tierra alta
(era el llanto callado)
son los campos de España.

Pero el desvanecimiento de la palabra "España" y de la realidad que nombra no supone el fin del sentimiento de destierro sino, aunque pueda parecer paradójico, su intensificación. Al margen ya de España, el poeta llega a sentir el destierro como privación absoluta, radical carencia expresada una y otra vez en palabras recurrentes que llevan en sí mismas la noción de ausencia o falta de algo: "silencio", "sombra", "soledad". Despojado de todo, el poeta es también ausencia él mismo, vacío, ni siquiera voluntad, apenas deseo inoperante: "Inmóvil, yo también soy sombra hambrienta...". En la obra de Luis Rius, la palabra emblemática "sombra" no sólo define el ámbito sin luz en el que el poeta habita, sino que acaba expresando la inconsistente materia de su ser.

La palabra "mar", una de las más reiteradas en la poesía de Luis Rius, portadora casi siempre de significaciones simbólicas muy especiales, es un inmejorable exponente de las mutaciones y desplazamientos que experimenta en su obra el tema del destierro, núcleo generador de su más intenso y personal mundo lírico.

En el primer libro de Rius, *Canciones de vela*, publicado en 1951, el mar representa el hondo y amargo foso que separa al poeta de lo que añora: y esa realidad que está al otro lado, aunque no nombrada con precisión, puede y debe identificarse todavía con la patria perdida e inalcanzable:

Otra vez frente al mar,
con mi frente abrasada
y mis ojos inmóviles, lejanos,
buscando sus espaldas.

El mar, como símbolo, cobra ambigüedad cuando desaparece la referencia a lo que está en la otra orilla. En *Canciones de amor y sombra*, libro de 1965, eso ya no importa; lo que importa es *el espacio en el que permanece la vida*, limitada y definida por la misteriosa e insondable presencia que el mar connota ahora:

De mar a mar, de campo a campo, ciega
la vida permanece
sin gozar ni sufrir,
sin memoria ni tiempo, indiferente.

Si antes el poeta, apelando a su destierro, podía alegar un destino excepcional, diferente al de la mayoría de los hombres, ahora refiere su angustia a una existencia sin atributos, "indiferente", despojada de todo lo que le conferiría intensidad y valor. La desolación obedece a otras causas, y el mar que la simbolizaba se convierte necesariamente en otra cosa, como afirma uno de los poemas de su último libro, *Canciones a Pilar Rioja* (1970):

> Si la distancia solamente fuese
> el mar extenso en medio de dos cuerpos,
> un barco haría el amor para surcarla.
> Pero no es sólo el mar, distancia es tiempo
> que es más grande que el mar, no permanece,
> como el espacio, inmóvil, va creciendo,
> distancia más distante todavía. . .

Esos versos explican la evolución y el sentido último del mundo de Luis Rius; si mar equivalía a espacio y distancia, la distancia acaba transfigurándose en tiempo. Ahí, en ese espacio inaprensible, dinámico, creciente, más amenazador que el mismo mar—al fin y al cabo, transitable—, es donde el poeta se siente confinado: "desterrado en el tiempo/ como en isla infinita,/ sin retorno. . .". No la carencia de una patria, sino el desamparo que se deriva de la pérdida irreparable del tiempo, será lo que decide la precariedad y la inutilidad de la existencia:

> Lo que viví ya pasó,
> lo que vivo está pasando,
> lo demás nunca llegó.
> Tan inútil mi vida
> como una raya
> dibujada en la arena
> al pie del agua.

Así, en el universo poético de Luis Rius, el exilio acaba configurándose como una experiencia inherente a la condición humana exenta de cualquier connotación socio-política. Esa marginación de lo histórico puede ser una razón más que explique el relativo desinterés con que su obra fue recibida por los lectores de un lado y otro del Atlántico, tan condicionados en su día por las tensiones de la Historia. Desaparecidas o reducidas las tensiones, cuando esa historia haya pasado definitivamente a la Historia, es de esperar que la poesía de Luis Rius se beneficie de su a-historicidad, y encuentre al fin los lectores que le negó su tiempo.

Notas

1 Ferres, Antonio y Ortega, José. *Literatura española del último exilio*. Gordian Press, New York, 1975, p. 8.

2 Rius, Luis. "Poesía española de México", *Revista de la Universidad de México*, v. 21, núm. 5, enero, 1967: 12-16.

3 Marra-López, José Ramón. "Jóvenes poetas españoles en México", *Insula*, núm. 222, mayo, 1965: 5.

4 González, Angel. Prólogo a *Cuestión de amor y otros poemas*, poesía completa de Luis Rius. Promexa, México, 1984, p. 8.

5 Francisco Carrasquer. "El exilio de la literatura y la literatura del exilio", *Camp de l'arpa*, no. 42, marzo, 1977.

TIERRA Y EXILIO EN JOSEP CARNER

Jaume Ferran
Syracuse University

Metimna, atrafegada, com mou la cara encesa
damunt el voleiar dels bracos i el vestit.
El dinar es cou, es veu lluir la roba estesa
i ja a la cantonada és Licas, el marit.

Es el comienzo del poema "Les llimones casolanes"—"Los limones caseros"—del primer libro de Josep Carner: "Els fruits saborosos"—"Los frutos sabrosos".

Como frutas sabrosas las palabras de Josep Carner sorprendían por su jugosidad a toda una generación y le marcaban, en la poesía, un camino: el novecentista. Traduzcámoslas:

Metimna, atareada, la faz mueve encendida
sobre el volar de brazos y vestido.
La comida se cuece, luce ropa estendida
y por la esquina asoma ya, Licas, el marido.

No nos engañemos. Los nombres de Metimna y de Licas—de indudable sabor clásico—aluden a criaturas de todos los días. Los frutos son los que Carner encuentra por doquier en los huertos catalanes. En ellos tenemos, viva y fragante, la mejor emanación de la tierra, de la única tierra que cantará Carner toda su vida: la tierra catalana.

Mirémosla con él. En uno de sus primeros retornos a Cataluña, él que a ella retornaría tantas veces nos dice:

Ja veig damunt la serra de foc el nostre pi
Oh gent que per les feixes daurades feu camí!
em sobta com un vi
la forca tota vella i humil que ens agermana.
(Es viu com la ginesta i com el blau marí
el teu escarafall, oh noia catalana)

Com somrieu en hores del vespre, masos blancs,
entre pallers de bona companyia,
i cada mas ateny en curta rodalia
bosquet i blat i vinya i un marge amb tres pollancs.

Voldria, tot perdent-me per valls i fondalades
dir tes llaors, oh terra de salut!
enmig de coses fosques i vides oblidades
com aquest grill que canta dins un camí perdut.

Traduzcamos también éste.

Retorno a Cataluña

Veo sobre la sierra de fuego nuestro pino
¡Oh, gente que por hazas doradas va en camino!
súbita, como un vino
la vieja fuerza humilde nos hermana.
(Vivo es cual la ginesta, cual el azul marino
tu aspaviento, muchacha catalana)

Sonreís en el poniente, oh caseríos blancos,
entre pajares que dan buena compañía,
sobre un corto contorno reina cada masía
de bosque y trigo y viña y un margen con tres álamos.

¡Quisiera yo al perderme por valles y hondonadas
decir tus alabanzas, oh tierra salutífera!
entre casas oscuras y vidas olvidadas
cual el grillo que canta en la senda perdida.

En este retorno de volver y de volver a ver, tenemos una primer y mágica instancia de visión de una tierra que se identifica indeleblemente con la femineidad, al final de la primera estrofa, en un paréntesis que destaca la imagen fundamental que enlaza a la tierra y a la muchacha catalana. . . Pertenece al libro *Bella terra, bella gent*.

Sí, la tierra es el escenario fundamental en el que transcurre la poesía de Josep Carner, el soporte natural de un mundo, que busca en la tierra, en lo telúrico, el asiento de todas las emociones. Y, no lo olvidemos; otro gran poeta—Pablo Neruda—lo ha dicho:

> "Los clásicos los produce la tierra o, más bien, la alianza entre sus libros y la tierra."[1]

En 1906, año de aparición de "Els fruits saborosos", Cataluña se abre a la contemporaneidad:

“En efecto, en este año se celebra el primer Congreso Internacional de la Lengua Catalana, con la participación de unos tres mil congresistas; se forma la “Solidaritat Catalana”, que arrastra a grandes masas de población en sus actos públicos; se publica *La Nacionalitat Catalana*, de Prat de la Riba, que se convierte en libro de cabecera de la burguesía nacionalista; se inicia la aparición cotidiana del *Glossari*, de Eugenio d‘Ors, que recogía—y elaboraba en doctrina—todas las inquietudes culturales de la época; y, finalmente, se editan una serie de obras literarias entre ellas *Els fruit soborosos*, de Josep Carner—que significan el final de una época y el inicio de otra.”[2]

Las palabras de Castellet y Molas sitúan la época y el libro en el marco exacto. Estábamos en el umbral del “noucentisme” o “novecentismo”. En Cataluña, como en Italia, donde se usaría la misma denominación, se sentía el estremecimiento de una nueva era y las “palpitaciones de los tiempos” pasaban por el tamiz orsiano para penetrar en un cuerpo social especialmente ávido de establecer un nuevo ritmo, esencialmente europeo.

En el momento en que Carner, en sus primeros libros, exalta la tierra, empieza el reino de la ciudad. La montaña, en el título y en el libro de su querido Guerau de Liost, es una “montaña de amatistas.” El mensaje de d’Ors es insoslayable:

> Catalanes, vamos a construir una ciudad. La historia es la génesis de la ciudad. . .
>
> . . .Cuando la piedra se ha convertido en mármol, y cuando el mármol empieza a adquirir conciencia de que es mármol, nace la *Civilidad*.[3]

Nadie más entusiasta que el joven Carner. Todos sus esfuerzos se decantarán hacia este cometido. Pero para ello no tendrá que renunciar a la tierra. Por ello, a pesar de los nombres clásicos veíamos en sus personajes a los que pueblan la tierra catalana, alargando sus manos ávidas hacia las frutas más sabrosas de nuestra tierra y de nuestra literatura. . .

El procedimiento nos pone en contacto con una constante del carácter catalán que Carner utiliza con eficacia: la ironía.

La ironía, como nos ha recordado Bajtín, es un arma del hombre moderno contra la grandilocuencia, constituyéndose en uno de los cauces de la que Carlos Bousoño ha llamado la minilocuencia. Sabe el hombre contemporáneo que no hay que elevarse demasiado para no llamar indebidamente la atención—como ocurre con los aviones modernos, si quieren evitar el radar. Para ello nada mejor que la ironía.

Entremos, con el poeta, en el jardín de una "quinta de arrabal".

Geraniums sechs. Acacias malaltissas
Tauletas de cafe.
Cinch testos gotejants, pintats de mangre,
y un banch pintat de vert.

El bon home s'ha tret l'americana
sobre el migrat roser
e inclina un poch demunt del llibre
son coll gros y rojench.

"Viatjes per las selvas africanas"
oh Stanley! oh valents!
Tropical sobre un bech de regadora
un raig de sol lluheix.

Geranios secos. Acacias enfermizas.
mesitas de café.
Cinco tiestos goteantes pintados con almagre,
banco de verde fiel.

El buen hombre se quita la chaqueta
bajo el escuálido rosal
y sobre el libro se inclina un tanto
su cuello grande que rojo está.

"Viajes por las selvas africanas"
¡Oh Stanley! ¡Oh valor!
Sobre la regadera, tropical
luce un rayo de sol.

Esta ironía que se advierte primordialmente en sus poemas iniciales, no dejará de acompañarle durante toda la vida. Podríamos llamarla "ironía reveladora", con la expresión de Josep Ferrater i Mora y siempre la encontramos unida al humor, según Miguel Arimany, que nos ha recordado la definición de la ironía que nos da el propio Carner en los versos siguientes:

sos codols suavitza la fresca fontanella
talment com la ironia poleix un esperit

la fresca fuentecilla suaviza sus cantos
tal como la ironía el espíritu pule,

En el marco del "novecentismo", que Xenius predicara con la solemnidad que le era habitual, la ironía carneriana que podría definirse como "la creencia a medias", para usar una expresión del mismo Xenius, es una de las armas más eficaces, entre tantas que se aprestan a levantar "La ciutat d'ivori"—La ciudad de marfil, como la llamara otro de los puntales del "novecentismo": su amigo Guerau de Liost.

Sin embargo, Carner será el máximo paladín del nuevo movimiento y a lo largo del siglo—oponiéndose ostensiblemente al barroco modernismo anterior—se va construyendo esta ciudad ideal, a la que los escritores aportan la máxima norma, pero en la que colaboran todos los trabajadores del espíritu.

Durante treinta años esta ciudad no hace más que crecer y reclamar nuevas avenidas resplandecientes; con ella, dentro de ella, crece irrefrenable la obra de Carner, que pronto adquiere un tono diamantino—Riba lo definirá como una "objetivación lírica",—que le permite marcar el camino que seguirá indeleble la mejor poesía de nuestro siglo.

La vida de Carner busca nuevos horizontes fuera de Cataluña desde 1921. Se los ofrece la carrera consular, que ejerce en Génova, en San José de Costa Rica, en El Havre, en Hendaya, sin que en ningún momento los avatares de su carrera diplomática pudieran alejar a Carner de aquella ciudad cuyos cimientos había puesto con los mejores y en la que no cesaba de colaborar, desde todas las esquinas que le deparaba su vida trashumante, que tras el breve paso por Ginebra—como asesor de la OIT de la Sociedad de Naciones—le conduce a Beirut... El hilo umbilical que le unía a Cataluña es más fuerte que nunca, como lo demuestra el libro que publica en 1935: "La primavera al poblet"—"La primavera en el pueblecillo"—.

Todo se lo llevaría la guerra civil, que le sorprende en el Líbano, pasando a la Embajada de Bruselas durante la guerra y terminando su carrera de diplomático—fiel a la República—como consejero de la Embajada española en París. . .

Aquella ciudad soñada se había venido estrepitosamente abajo: "la guerra lo destrozó todo. Este es un suceso que me partió por la mitad, un veritable desastre", confesó a Porcel.[4]

Sí. La guerra civil, que había partido a España en dos partía también por la mitad la vida del poeta, que ahora sí, encontraba en el exilio una nueva perspectiva amarga, dramática, que pronto se reflejaría en uno de sus libros fundamentales: *Nabí*, aparecido en 1941, que parece que "Fue concebido en Hendaya, continuado en Beirut, donde Carner fue cónsul un año y medio (1935-36), y terminado en México",[5] como nos recuerda Gabriel Ferrater.

Es importante la precisión ferrateriana, porque nos damos cuenta de que el poeta había ido tomando una progresiva toma de conciencia frente a un mundo que se desmoronaba a su alrededor.

En este descenso al Hades—que era, al tiempo, un descenso a lo más hondo de su propio ser—encuentra Carner de nuevo la tierra, que ve con los ojos del primer hombre:

> La terra que et portava enorgullida
> Adam, hereu del mon, mai no t'oblida;

La tierra, que le llevaba enorgullecida, no podía olvidar a Adán, el heredero del mundo, como la tierra catalana no olvidaba al "Príncipe" de sus poetas—como se le había llamado desde la juventud—ahora errante en México, donde la llevaba con él y tornaba a arraigar, más que nunca, en su poesía.

Era una vuelta a la tierra, a la raíz, a las raíces. No nos extraña que uno de los mejores libros de Carner, en el año 1953, al demediar su exilio, se llamara *Arbres*—"Arboles". Si cuando tenía la tierra su amor por ella la evocaba en los frutos sabrosos que le ofrecía, ahora, que la tierra le faltaba la buscaba cantando los árboles que en ella crecen.

Pablo Neruda ha dicho:

> "Las tierras de la frontera metieron sus raíces en mi poesía y nunca han podido salir de ella. Mi vida es una larga peregrinación que siempre da vueltas, que siempre retorna al bosque austral, a la selva".[6]

También es una larga peregrinación, por los caminos de la diáspora española, la vida de Carner, que, huérfano de su tierra, la ve crecer en los árboles, que recuerda.

El mismo poeta traduce el poema "Arboles" y nos da una visión imperecedora de los viejos compañeros de los hombres, diciendo:

> Para mi corazón
> árbol, quisiera tu saber que te hace
> paciente en días arrecidos,
> pródigo, en tiempo ardiente, de tesoros.[7]

Arbres sería el primer libro de Carner que tras la guerra se editaba en Cataluña. El próximo serían las *Obres Completes* con las que la Editorial Selecta devolvía a Cataluña su máximo poeta, en toda la amplitud de su obra "revivida" a la manera de Juan Ramón Jiménez, con quien le ha comparado acertadamente Pere Cimferrer diciendo:

> "Se trata, en cierto sentido, de dos trayectorias paralelas:

dados a conocer muy jóvenes, extraordinariamente virtuosos y virtuosistas en su oficio, ambos poetas supusieron, en el momento de su irrupción, un cambio decisivo en las respectivas literaturas".[8]

El poeta Manuel Durán, en cambio, prefiere compararlo con Jorge Guillén:

> "El temperamento abierto y positivo, en ambos casos, se profundiza al abrirse a un doble amor, los clásicos hispanos—castellanos, catalanes—y los grandes modernos, franceses e ingleses, especialmente, pero sin excluir otras grandes culturas".[9]

Tanto si le comparamos con Juan Ramón Jiménez, como si lo hacemos con Jorge Guillén, Carner nos presta una personalidad paralela en las letras catalanas, que tuvieron en él alguien que dio una nueva avenida a nuestra poesía, ampliando los caminos que habían desbrozado eficazmente Verdaguer y Maragall. . .

También se parece a ambos en formar parte de aquella "España peregrina", como fue definida por José Bergamín, que llevó lo mejor de España por el mundo, hasta que, desde el exilio, tornan a mirar hacia el origen, hacia los orígenes, a los que no han sabido renunciar a pesar del alejamiento. . .

En el poema "al alma" de su último libro *El tomb de l'anny*—El giro del año—dice el poeta:

> Sota la nit espesseida i crua,
> escric, terra pairal, en ta llaor;
>
> Bajo la noche espesa y cruda, escribo
> para alabarte, tierra de mis padres

No hizo otra cosa Carner a lo largo de toda su vida. Tanto en la primera época, que transcurre en el ámbito encantado de su tierra natal—y que culmina en la Antología *La inútil ofrena*—La inútil ofrenda, como después soñándola desde la lejanía diplomática o el exilio político, cuando sus sueños de amante alejado avivan si cabe los perfiles de la tierra que había dejado atrás. . .

Toda la obra de Carner es un canto o un retorno a la tierra, que en uno de sus poemas ve "De lluny estant"—Desde lejos:

> Qui veiés, quan l'estiu s'acomiada,
> el camí—la serp blanca i somrient—
> i, al marge d'una cala refiada

el pámpol mort sota d'un pi vivent.

Qui veiés una dansa damunt l'era
i una serra morada enlla de mi;
qui topés un aloc de torrentera
o enmig d'un pedruscall, un romaní.

Més val, pero, que a aquests bedolls s'aca
el meu esment, i a aauest boiram somort.
En mos camins d'un temps, hom pot trobar-h
un angel trist amb el seu glavi tort.

Quien viera al tiempo en que el verano acaba
el camino—la sierpe blanca y riente—
y en la orilla de cada confiada
la muerta vid bajo el pino viviente.

Quien un baile mirara sobre la era
y una morada sierra allá a lo lejos;
quien encontrara un fruto en torrentera
o, en medio de las piedras, un romero.

Pero es mejor que mi atención se centre
en estos abedules, nieblas calmas.
En mis sendas de antaño, puede verse
un ángel triste con torcida espada.

Impresiona la nitidez de la evocación, en la que Carner es siempre maestro, pero el poeta no puede, no quiere engañarse y se pregunta en uno de los sonetos de su libro *Llunyania*—Lejanía:

Pero qui lluny del tros nadiu s'enllara
com pervindria a un absolut retorn?

Pero quien lejos de su tierra vive
como podrá del todo retornar?

Es una pregunta que no le abandona, sobre todo en sus últimos años cuando el poeta se encuentra—y lo dice con un verso de Jordi de Sant Jordi,

Desert d'amics, de béns i de senyor
Sin amigos, sin bienes ni señor[10]

Es el mismo Carner, que en los años cuarenta había conocido Manuel Durán en Méjico, cuando "Era, ante todo, una inmediata presencia llena de alegría, de esperanza, de optimismo".[11] Era el mismo, pero había pasado por el infierno del exilio—que lo es mucho más, si cabe, para el escritor que depende de una atmósfera, de un clima que sólo su país le proporciona—y que no debemos confundir con la lengua, que, al menos, le acompaña. . .

En una de las vueltas y revueltas del exilio había vuelto a Bruselas, aquella ciudad a la que había llegado en el cenit de su carrera diplomática el 29 de agosto de 1936 y en la que había conocido a su segunda esposa, Emilie Noulet, la conocida crítica y profesora, especialista en el simbolismo francés. En Bruselas soñó un día que allí mismo le gustaría envejecer, en un poema, cuyo título es:

BELGICA

Si fossin el meu fat les terres estrangeres,
m'agradaria fer-me vell en un país
on es filtrés la llum, grisa i groga, en somrís
i hi hagués prades amb ulls d'aigua i amb voreres
guarnides d'arcos, d'oms i de pereres.
. . . .
Si fuesen mi destino las tierras extranjeras
quisiera envejecer en un país
que filtrara en sonrisa la luz dorada y gris
y donde hubiera márgenes y agua en las praderas
de espinos, olmos y perales llenas.
. . . .

Los poetas no mienten, ni siquiera al soñar. Josep Carner moriría en Bélgica, como César Vallejo había de morir en París "con aguacero". Todavía pudo retornar, una vez más,—una sola vez—a su querida Cataluña en 1970. . . Yo estaba en Barcelona el día de su llegada y no pude recibirle—como tantos de mis compatriotas lo hicieron—porque me había detenido en un periódico para que mis palabras no faltaran aquella tarde entre las que le daban la bienvenida. Nada he sentido tanto como aquella ausencia mía, que ahora no me permite recordarle como tantos le vieron, como la última encarnación de una Cataluña, que con su llegada tornaba a anunciarse y florecer. Con lo que, si bien se mira, la indomeñable esperanza y optimismo que en él detectara Manuel Durán años antes en Méjico, no dejaban de acompañarle. Pero su destino era morir en Bélgica entre los espinos, olmos y perales que le acompañaron en su exilio, recordando sin duda los árboles de su tierra catalana, cuyos frutos sabrosos había cantado un día en su primer, gran libro. . .

Notes

[1] Pablo Neruda, *Para nacer he nacido*. Seix Barral Biblioteca Breve, Barcelona, 1978, p. 88.

[2] *Ocho siglos de poesía catalana*. Antología bilingüe. El libro de bolsillo, Alianza Editorial, Madrid, p. 24.

[3] Jaime Ferrán, *Antología Eugenio d'Ors*. Doncel, 8, Madrid, 1967, pp. 17 y siguientes. En ellas se recoge la doctrina orsiana de la Civilidad, base del movimiento "noucentista".

[4] Albert Manent, *Tres escritores catalanes: Carner, Riba, Pla*. Gredos, S.A. Madrid 1973, p. 190.

[5] Josep Carner, *Nabí*. Barcelona, Edicions 62, 1970, p. 21.

[6] Pablo Neruda, lib. cit., p. 201.

[7] *Cuadernos del Congreso por la libertad de la cultura*, Marzo-Abril, 1955, p. 61.

[8] "Permanencia de Josep Carner", *Revista "Destino"*, Barcelona 29, mayo, 1971, p. 58.

[9] Manuel Durán, "Josep Carner: Clasicismo, vitalismo, intimismo (y algo más)". *Cuadernos Hispanoamericanos*, 412, p. 6.

[10] *Josep Carner en els seus millors escrits, els dies i els homes II*. Editorial Miquel Arimany S.A. Barcelona, 1984. (Albert Manent, "Una aventura intel.lectual i vital", p. 21).

[11] Manuel Durán, *Op. cit.* p. 5.

WHAT IS NOT SAID IN
HISTORIAS E INVENCIONES DE FELIX MURIEL

Mary S. Gossy
Harvard University

In *Historias e invenciones de Félix Muriel*[1] Rafael Dieste creates a regime in which the civil war and the succeeding repression are themselves censored—any mention of either is absent from the book. This is not to say that Dieste has no opinions or preferences about what happened in Spain during and after the war. On the contrary, he was intimately involved in the cultural programs of the Republic, organizing and producing shows for the *Misiones pedagógicas*; among other projects he also wrote "Al amanecer", a propagandistic farce attacking societal forces supporting the old order. When war broke out he took up arms on the Republican side, survived the general slaughter, and kept up an almost twenty year long exile in the Americas in opposition to Franco's regime. Dieste's personal concern and sacrifice lead his reader to wonder why there are only two even vaguely political statements in *Félix Muriel* (33; 154), and absolutely no mention of the civil war, even though the book was published in 1943. It appeared at the seat of the author's exile, Buenos Aires, a scant five years after Dieste's departure from Spain—long before his or anybody else's wounds could have begun to heal.

But exclusion of an overt discussion of civil war events is not the same thing as authorial indifference. The absence of so large-looming a theme from so well-engineered a narrative does not hide the absent thing; it draws attention to it. Rafael Dieste's attitudes towards the civil war and its aftermath can be found, literally, between the lines. They are delineated by what is not there. The grandiose silence in *Félix Muriel* says as much as many words. Small wonder, then, that printed ellipses appear on almost every page of the book: those three dots are used more as words than as punctuation. . .

The negative images of the author's ideas may be found in the text in the form of an obsession with memory and forgetfulness. These two themes twine through the *Historias* from the first word of the title to the end of the last story. The fixation on the vanished and forgotten, attributed by some critics to a Gallego-Celtic fascination with fairies[2], is also and perhaps more emphatically a challenge to the reader to remember, and to dare to invoke the presence of wartime memories. The narrator's unwillingness to name them or remember them puts a burden of curiosity and memory on the reader.

By following the theme of forgetfulness through the *Historias*, the reader is able to come to an understanding of the importance of the unseen, unremembered, and unsaid in the book. It is easy to separate the two kinds of story found in the collection on the basis of content and form—but because of Dieste's penchant for ambiguity, it is almost impossible firmly to call one kind "historia" and the other "invención". By giving us the names of two varieties of narrative, Dieste has told us that both exist, but not where either begins or leaves off, or which name pertains to each kind. The only thing that is certain is that "story" is part of "history" (*historia* connotes both fiction and fact), that the artistic invention that is fiction is welded to the story of the past.

The book begins and ends with an intimate, first-person address to the reader from a narrating "I" that may be inferred (from its context in relation to characters from later stories, cf. p. 12) to be Félix Muriel's. Still, a personal voice is conspicously absent from the first two paragraphs of the book. They are purely descriptive and devoid of human activity. The "Quinqué color guinda", like the "happy bright sea" that is his namesake[3], illumines the first spaces that Félix sees. Because of it, the protagonist is able to see just enough; its diffuse light makes it possible for him to love the shape of space, of the world (11)—partly because its dimness veiled imperfections.

The real turf where all the events described in "El quinqué" take place is a landing on the staricase of Félix's childhood home. But the narrator makes it clear that none of them could have happened here had it not been for the *quinqué* and the light it shed. The story is told in past tenses, but creates the present by making things visible in the mild, warm light of the lamp. Its light is analogous to liquid: ". . .como un pequeño mar. . ." (11) and ". . .era un licor de amistad. . ." (12). Félix Muriel as narrator is born from the liquid and light that is "el quinqué". That light makes it possible for him to see, and to show and tell his reader what he sees.

The stories after "El quinqué" move from original clarity, recognition, and optimism, to an increasingly willful forgetfulness and ambiguity. In "Este niño está loco" little Félix runs from a dark salon filled with portraits of his ancestors to his father, who stands in the light at the end of the corridor approaching it. His aunt Eulalia, observing his career from her seat in a well-lit room where she reads historical romances, remarks, "Este niño está loco". (21) Why is he crazy? Because he tries, like his father who paces the distance without fear, to "ir y volver" (20) between the past and the present. In her safe place, Eulalia reads a fictionalized account of a distant past that has nothing to do with her present. Her contact with the past in the form of novelizations of court intrigues gives her an illusory control over it. Fictional history (like the *Historias e invenciones* themselves) is, paradoxically, a means to forgetfulness. Only a crazy kid would want to explore his dark personal past, to stand in the shadows of the almost-forgotten and try to see what is there.

In this second story Félix confronts, for the first time, forgetfulness as an option. It slowly begins to appear to be a desirable one after "Juana Rial", the third story. The voice telling this story is a little sour, is looking back over the years with a little more worldly experience than the nostalgic rememberer of "Este niño está loco". The entire long first paragraph is a disclaimer for the seriousness of what follows: "Eso me asusta un poco, pues la cosa no tiene esa importancia. Acaso tenga otra. . ." (25)

Wishful thinking. The story's importance is that it reminds us that we are all capable of unforgivable offenses. The narrator recounts the terrible saga of Juana Rial and her stoning by the populace of Félix's village, and of his own guilt in the matter. He only able to tell the story because he has (to his own partial satisfaction, but not to his reader's) utterly devalued its import in the first paragraph. Juana Rial's tragedy is her ostracism and death at the hands of the villagers. The narrator's tragedy is that the event "sirvió de leño a mi deslumbramiento". (25) The benificent dimness of the "quinqué" gives way to a blinding flash; he sees and knows too much: there is so much to see that he sees nothing. Dieste uses derivatives of "deslumbrar" twice in this brief story: in the sentence above, and at the end, when the narrator feels himself accused by "aquellas olas deslumbrantes" of "aquel mar imposible. . ." (29) of reality which he flees as fast as he can.

The memory that touches off the flight from remembrance that dominates the rest of the book can be distilled to this: A community under both internal and external pressure turns violently on one of its own number, and commits fratricide. There is such communal guilt after the crime that each individual wants to forget that it happened. The whole story might serve as a little exemplum of millions of parallel incidents of fratricide that occurred in the civil war. Dieste wrote his book in 1943, when fingers of blame were pointing in every direction. This story reminds its reader that only he who is without sin may cast a stone. But more than that, it emphasizes the difficulty of remembering the incident at all, the temptation to say it does not matter, that it is not important.

Still, there is no moral in the story—just the last words, "salí corriendo". (29) The instinct that makes Félix run becomes a conscious act of repression in "El loro disecado". In this story, where everybody ". . . tiene derecho al silencio. . ." (33) Félix becomes a willing accomplice to the conspiracy of silence that begins to dominate the mute spaces between the lines of the book. First, don Ramón invents silly lies about a parrot's origin for the amusement of his clientele; in fact, he is veiling a sordid personal story. Once, in the company of young Lisardo, he almost tells the truth, but instead covers up his slip (36). By the end of the story, Félix's knowledge of a little French makes him privy to don Ramón's secret confession to his father. Félix's father, on obtaining the assurance "—No diré nada" from his son, shakes his hand, "como a una persona mayor. Y yo primero no supe qué hacer. Pero después se la apreté también. Como don Ramón." (45) These are no longer schoolboy pranks. He is now initiated into the grey ranks of everyday adult compromise, complicity, and duplicity.

But Félix is going to have a hard time keeping his secrets: his memory is too good for his own good. Félix has shown us that the harder one tries to forget what he knows, the more difficult it becomes to avoid his knowledge. By trying very hard not to overhear his father and don Ramón's conversation, he heard. He says that putting so much attention on *not* paying attention paradoxically enables him to understand everything ". . .con sorprendente claridad." (38) By shaking hands with his father, Félix makes a pact of silence. But if he had kept his promise to his father how would the reader know the true story at all? It appears that Félix made a casuistic deal with himself, too: he will not *say* anything, but he will write it. This is what necessitates the change of person in the next and succeeding stories. "El jardín de Plinio" starts in the third person, shifts to first person during the intercalated story found in loose sheets by don Julián, then switches back to the third person and protracted dialogue. Félix agrees not only in intent but also in action to silence and deception. The story involves a silencing, or a censoring, of a voice of conscience inside. And when another person becomes party to this censorship, or even encourages it by silence, he assumes part of the guilt. That is the meaning of Félix's "Nuestra—. . ." (74) at the end of the story.

When Félix becomes an accomplice in the silent cover-ups, he is no longer able to remember in first-person as an eyewitness: he must "tell stories" in order to tell the truth. The idiomatic expression 'to tell stories' (i.e., to tell lies) is helpful here because it shows that Félix Muriel, the author of the story stuck in the middle of "El jardín", can only speak now through fiction, through his own stories. The next stories in the book, up to the change in the last, follow this pattern. To bring it into historical context, one might say that just as Félix is compelled to speak only the veiled half-truths of stories, Rafael Dieste in exile in Buenos Aires is constrained to speak his mind only through the life and work of his own storybook character, Félix Muriel, in a semi-mythologized world of quasi-exempla. There is safety in narrative distance—a fact proven from the works of S. Teresa and Cervantes to those of Dieste.

The next three stories have some of the attributes of exempla and saints' lives. Each has religious overtones and appears to teach a tiny, almost inscrutable lesson. Each one has metaliterary aspects, deals with marginalized, solitary people, and takes place in the context of the battle between remembering and forgetting. In addition, it seems that in these three stories Dieste is offering some remedies for forgetfulness. The characters fight themselves to acknowledge their pasts as their own, and manage by so doing to forgive themselves and others. This process of reconciliation takes place (after an introduction in the third person) in the form of a dialogue between the main characters of each story.

What the narrator seeks is what Anselmo talks about in the following passage:

> . . . de la virtud de un instante ahondado, nacerían otros, y ya no serían los mismos uno tras otros, como las letras de un texto inalterable. Pero la que he vivido es ya un texto inalterable y ni yo quería alterarlo, sino entrar en ella y salvarla; y si no puedo, pedir auxilio. (115)

A play on words at the end of "Carlomagno" makes it appear that the world was as much *written* as created by God. The final words of Carlomagno's last two utterances are:

> —. . .la escritura del Señor.
> —. . .la criatura del Señor. (130)

By this word play the narrator closely links the written with living creatures, suggesting that if creatures are written, perhaps they can be redeemed by writing and literature. This ideal, expressed at the end of the three idealized exempla/saints' lives, brings us to the last story of the book.

Unfortunately, "La asegurada" plants Félix back in the reality of conflict. Here he begins to reveal how intimately he became involved with the fate of Eloísa, and refers to his public as "vosotros", so that the narrative distance is the shortest possible. He addresses his story to a plural, familiar second person, not just to one individual—he is talking to a whole people. Once out of the world of the exempla, the reader discovers that he is also beyond the world of happy endings. Félix's inability to break his silence makes him, by his negligence, an accessory to Eloísa's death. With the understatement characteristic of confessions in his book, Félix says at first "Tal vez mi silencio fue lo más dañino" (153), but then tells the truth: "Pero no dije nada y la maté lo mismo. . ." (153) The consequence of his silence is that he can no longer see anything: ". . .no vi nada por mucho que abrí los ojos." (154) Blindness is as integral to this last story as being blinded by the light was to the first. The villagers watching Eloísa's mother and grandfather taking away her corpse "los perdieron de vista" (156). But the eyes of Félix Muriel as *narrator* permit the reader to see the story to its ambivalent end. Félix redeems himself and Eloísa at least partially by deciding to remember and to tell what he knows, addressing his readers as "vos", as in dialogue, that there might be communication, and perhaps a hint or the possibility of reconciliation. He tells his grandfather, the doctor, the truth of what happened to Eloísa in order to protect her memory (154)—and with a metaliterarily ironic overstatement, the doctor replies:

> —Con un papel sellado lo arreglaré todo. Ya me lo echarán en cara los conservadores cuando les toque gobernar. Pero ahora va para largo. Antes pienso estar bajo tierra. (154)

Writting can help matters, and even if the conservatives try to use the writing against its author, once the written is read, it's too late—the silence has been broken.

Rafael Dieste uses a panoply of shifts in narrative person, combined with an insistence on the theme of conflict between remembering and forgetting, to create a book with both personal and universal applications. His text stands as a witness to post-civil war Spain, challenging a nation to lift the interpersonal silence imposed by censorship, exile, and psychic and political repression; to admit the forgotten, to converse, to try to bring about some measure of reconciliation. Dieste's emphatic silence and his characters' conflicted forgetfulness drive the reader to remember and to speak.

Notes

[1] Rafael Dieste, *Historias e invenciones de Félix Muriel.* (Madrid: Alianza Editorial, 1974). Page numbers parenthesized in my text refer to this edition.

[2] Estelle Irizarry and Pere Gimferrer, among others, have noted the influence of folkloric imagery and symbolism in Dieste's work. See Irizarry's *Rafael Dieste* (Boston: Twayne/ G.K. Hall, 1979) for a full bibliography.

[3] The etymology of "muriel", "probably from a Celtic cognate of Irish *muirgheal*", is "bright sea" (American Heritage Dictionary). And of course "felix" is the Latin "happy".

CUANDO EL DOLOR SE VUELVE EXPERIENCIA: GERMAN BLEIBERG Y SU POESIA EN EL EXILIO

Chantal Cassan-Moudoud
Syracuse University

La selección de poemas publicada en 1975 y editada por Germán Bleiberg [1] agrupa en el último apartado a poemas escritos entre 1952 y 1973 o sea, fuera de España. Como lo subrayó Inman Fox en un symposium celebrado en 1968 en Syracuse,[2] la selección, ordenación y revisión de su poesía es una de las preocupaciones del poeta contemporáneo ya que quiere dar al lector "no una colección o antología, sino un verdadero libro de poesía que lleva al lector—o al mismo poeta—por un mundo lírico completo y acabado."[3] Es en ese mundo, tal como lo ordenó Germán Bleiberg, que buscaré las huellas dejadas en su poesía por la experiencia del exilio.

Los once poemas escritos fuera de España y agrupados bajo el título *Poemas*,[4] son una continuación de la problemática desarrollada por Bleiberg en su obra anterior. Pero los sentimientos expresados se visten de un sentido especial y sobre todo llevan al poeta a conclusiones diferentes ya que la situación de la cual emanan es totalmente diferente.

Los poemas escritos en la cárcel[5] revelaban la angustia de una persona que sabe que no es maestra de su destino. La felicidad del recordar alternaba con el deseo de olvidar para no sufrir más y con la nostalgia, a medio camino entre esos dos polos.

En los poemas que nos ocupan, los mismos sentimientos aparecen pero esta vez la cárcel no es tanto un elemento exterior como una actitud: hay la misma búsqueda de libertad. El exilio físico tiene su paralelo en el exilio mental que experimenta el poeta. El poeta vive en otro mundo, vive en sus recuerdos y esa serie de poemas nos muestra el itinerario seguido por Bleiberg hacia el "bienaventurado albergue" de su último poema.

El poema que abre la sección *Poemas*, es una elegía: "Elegía en la muerte de Pedro Salinas", que acaba de morir en exilio en Puerto Rico. La elegía empieza por una cita de Garcilaso que alude a la separación física del poeta y de su país:

> La mar en medio y tierras he dejado (p. 71)

Los temas de la muerte y del recuerdo se encuentran otra vez forzosamente reunidos. La obra del Poeta, escrita al ritmo del recuerdo, sobrevive al poeta-hombre y se vuelve poesía-vida:

> el poeta sigue viviendo o tal vez duerma,
> lejanamente dormido en su vigilia,
> siempre sin morir nunca. (p. 72)

En ese poema Bleiberg ha concentrado todo el sentido de una vida de poeta, ese deseo de sobrevivir su propia muerte. El poema "Oración a la muerte", publicado en 1936, y escogido por Bleiberg para abrir su libro, vuelve a la memoria del lector. En ese poema el poeta exponía sus sentimientos hacia la muerte: vista al principio como una limitación, la muerte se hacía "tránsito" que iba a permitir al poeta "rescatar las horas perdidas".[6] Al escoger la "Elegía en la muerte de Pedro Salinas" para abrir la última sección de sus poemas, Bleiberg establece un paralelismo con ese poema. Pero, si todavía se ve la muerte como un "dulce tránsito breve" se nota entre la oración y la elegía todo el peso de lo que se ha vuelto irremediablemente experiencia vivida y ya no esfuerzo intelectual de entender el sentido del recuerdo y del olvido. El poeta ha cambiado. Como lo escribía en un verso de "El amor y el paisaje," ha visto el "dolor convertido en experiencia" (p. 21).

En "Baile de Navidad," el segundo poema de esa sección, reaparece el tema de la soledad ya experimentada en la cárcel. Los mismos sentimientos vuelven, las mismas soluciones: la vuelta a su ser íntimo y a su soledad, pero esta vez la cárcel es el exilio.

En el poema siguiente, "Vigilia", la soledad se ha vuelto aislamiento. El sentimiento nacido en la cárcel encuentra otra vez su expresión:

> Esta puerta, tal vez cerrada al viento.
> Todo parece—¿contra quién?—cerrado.
> Hasta las nubes de la lejanía,
> horizontal penumbra, y tantas rejas
> ventanales hostiles. (p. 75)

Pero ahora el poeta sabe que él, sólo, puede liberarse de esa cárcel:

> (La puerta, tan sencilla como el campo,
> nadie ha intentado abrirla, y veo sangre

como espejos, amor hacia paredes,
hacia siempre, mi sangre inútil, tuya)
La puerta cede y todo es mío, (p. 75)

Con ese poema se anuncia un cambio de actitud hacia la muerte: la muerte se vuelve controlable. El sentimiento que el poeta puede enfrentar hasta cierto punto empieza a nacer. En el poema siguiente, "Origen", escribe:

Os lo había dicho la otra tarde:
la primavera no parece igual para todos nosotros.
Para mí ha de ser mucho más corta.
No pertenezco a esa hilera de soñolientos peregrinos.
Mi primavera durará el tiempo de mirarse a los ojos
o de reclinarse sobre el alma en silencio. (p. 77)

Y concluye muy claramente:

Es de noche y cuando quiera madrugar hacia mi primavera
sabré que soy distinto, que soy mío, distinto, hasta un muerte
[muy distinto] (p. 77)

El después de la muerte ha vuelto a ser primavera, renacer.

Tres años después escribe un poema de tonalidad muy diferente: "Hay tantos muertos en mi corazón. . ." El sentimiento de poder decidir ha desaparecido, la angustia de morir sin haber acabado el camino interior del recuerdo vuelve a aparecer:

No me dejes morir con tantos muertos
cuando hay nieve tan pura en algún horizonte
no me dejes con tantos muertos en el corazón. (p. 78)

El poema siguiente, titulado "La visita," es una larga composición muy emocionante en la que el poeta recibe al fin la visita tan anhelada y en la que ya no creía: la nostalgia, antecámara del olvido, visitadora de los años carcelarios, ha vuelto a visitar al poeta. Es la única ahora que lo pueda acompañar:

Dejaremos que empiece a cubrirnos la nieve
sabemos los dos que estamos fuera
sencillamente en el camino
confundiendo palabras con besos
desterrados del tiempo y de las lágrimas
echando de menos tal vez algún terrenal abismo. (p.79)

A esta larga composición siguen cinco poemas titulados "Buffalo" y en los cuales, siguiendo el ritmo ya establecido en la poesía anterior, domina el silencio. Pero esta vez es, quizás, un silencio más sarcástico ya que no impide la resurgencia de la memoria. Pero es una memoria exterior, fabricada: las fechas, los datos históricos. . .

En el último de los dos poemillas de "Buffalo" se precisa aun más ese sentimiento de desengaño frente al recuerdo:

> Porque pensar en los ríos
> . . . .
> todo se sumirá en historia mal sabida
> nada se sabrá al fin (p.87)

El recuerdo tan celebrado se ha mostrado al poeta tal como es: un engaño.

El último poema del libro, "Pensaba todos los días," es la conclusión de la obra de Bleiberg. Encabezado por dos versos de Góngora, el poema nos anuncia que el poeta encontró al fin una solución, ha encontrado el "albergue" deseado.

En ese poema, Bleiberg demuestra otra vez su capacidad de superar las más hondas desesperaciones y su optimismo fundamental en la fuerza de la vida. Desde su primer poema, "Oración a la muerte," había presentido esa felicidad pero la situaba después de la muerte. En una visión intelectual de la existencia no se había dado cuenta de que se podía gozar del momento presente. La cárcel, con todo lo que implica de autodefensa para no dejarse alienar totalmente, no le permitió encontrar la solución. Pero, el exilio, al hacer vivir el poeta otra vez en un mundo rodeado por el recuerdo, pero sin las presiones de la cárcel, le permite llegar a ese descubrimiento.

La primera estrofa del poema es un resumen de toda esa vida consagrada al sueño:

> Pensaba todos los días
> mes tras mes: ¡Qué larga es la noche! (p.88)

Pero ahora se da cuenta de que:

> y ha bastado simplemente
> alzar los párpados (p. 88)

Es una nueva vida que se abre ante él. La necesidad de buscar siempre ha desaparecido:

> Ya no pienso en las sombras
> de la noche larga. (p. 88)

En un final lleno de profunda serenidad, el poeta dice adiós para siempre a la amarga nostalgia. La "puerta amarilla" está al fin abierta, nuevos horizontes se abren.

Una intuición temprana expresada en la "Oración a la muerte" se encontró actualizada, bien a pesar del poeta. La experiencia carcelaria y la del exilio ampliaron esa temática dándole un sentido trágico y forzando al poeta a encontrar la quietud en el olvido, muerte hasta cierto punto del poeta. A la cárcel física correspondió la cárcel que se hizo el poeta con sus recuerdos, y al exilio físico correspondió el exilio definitivo de sus recuerdos.

Notas

[1] German Bleiberg, *Selección de poemas (1936-1973)* (London: Grant & Cutler, 1975). Todos los poemas citados siguen la paginación de esa edición.

[2] Inman Fox, "German Bleiberg, poeta de la existencia" in *Symposium*, Summer 1968, 153-163.

[3] Ibid, p. 155.

[4] El libro *Selección de poemas (1936-1973)* reúne los poemas escritos antes de la guerra: "Oración a la muerte" y los "Sonetos amorosos," los poemas escritos durante los años carcelarios e inmediatamente al salir de la cárcel, y los poemas escritos fuera de España. Los poemas escritos entre 1936 y 1945 habían sido publicado juntos bajo el título *Más allá de las ruinas*. En la selección German Bleiberg no volvió a publicar todos los poemas publicados bajo ese título.

[5] "Más allá de las ruinas," "El amor y el paisaje", p. 21.

[6] "Oración a la muerte", p. 3.

LA EXPERIENCIA ARGENTINA: PARA CONMEMORAR EL CENTESIMO ANIVERSARIO DEL NACIMIENTO DE RICARDO GUIRALDES (1886-1986)

CUADERNO DE BITACORA DE *DON SEGUNDO SOMBRA*

Alberto Blasi
CUNY Graduate Center &
Brooklyn College

No poseemos una memoria, un cuaderno de bitácora que nos permita seguir el camino del escritor durante la producción de *Don Segundo Sombra*. Sin embargo, sus cartas a un colega y padrino en letras, algunas de su mujer, y un diario personal tomado y dejado en tres momentos distintos de su vida, proveen alguna luz sobre aquel intrincado proceso. Ensamblados con precaución los fragmentos que hacen al tema en las tres fuentes enunciadas y cotejándolos con otros documentos de época se puede construir una secuencia supletoria de aquella carencia indicada al principio. Es lo que se trata de hacer en las páginas que siguen. En su mayoría, los materiales utilizados para ello son inéditos.

El primer testimonio, en términos de cronología es de diciembre de 1919 y habla de una profunda desorientación[1]; ha sometido sus textos a un influyente mediador y por entonces muy respetado crítico y le dice: "todo lo que se ha dicho y dejado de decir sobre mi personalidad literaria, me ha desorientado bastante y espero de su opinión un poco de luz". Es sobradamente conocida la malandanza crítica y editorial de los primeros libros de Güiraldes para que esta dramática aserción necesite ser clarificada. En enero de 1920 le dice en otra carta: "La ciudad, en el fondo me es antipática (. . .) Culpe Ud. de este modo arbitrario de juzgar a mi costumbre y amor por la pampa, con su sol, su aire, y la exaltación individual que crea. (. . .) Lluvias y brumas están dando a mi pobre individuo una palidez aguachenta de hongo." Esta opción a favor del campo y en contra de la ciudad será una invariante en su espíritu tal como lo prueba su diatriba contra Buenos Aires de 1925: "Estoy cansado de esta ciudad sin alma. . ." (1962: 769). Ambas cartas fueron escritas en París, de allí pasó a Mallorca; luego de un mes en la isla, en marzo de 1920 desde Puerto Pollensa escribe a su amigo francés: hace una larga y admirada descripción del lugar y de sus gentes y, referido a los numerosos pintores que trabajan en la isla, asienta: "Yo los envidio un poco pues lo que quisiera hacer no lo encontraré ni en la montaña ni en las calas y estoy, por el momento, como un pobre sediento echando el balde en una cisterna vacía. Malos momentos son éstos que uno debe dejar pasar sin neurastenia. No tema Ud. Estoy muy lejos de ella. Para mí el escribir es una resultante de la vida. No tengo pues por qué afligirme de estar gozando a nervios abiertos." Esta relación entre experiencia y textualización, entre vida vivida y operación artística, es otra de sus invariantes, generosamente documentada por Victoria Ocampo (1941: 289-327); Blasi 1970: 13-15) mientras que el diario inédito del escritor enriquece y ejemplifica minuciosamente el tema (Blasi 1982: 21-29). En otra carta, de julio de 1920, habla de la que llama "generación francesa de 1870 a 1900" y confiesa: "Mi admiración por ella ha sido tan violenta que me consideraba feliz de ser algo así como un pobre pozo oscuro, cuya agua, en el mediodía, se hacía luz por reflejo. Para mí, los escritores se dividen en dos grupos: los que han querido a aquella generación, y los que han pasado a la vera de un milagro, sin sentirlo mejor que un buey." Aquí nuevamente el establecimiento de otra opción que se construirá en una invariante como lo corrobora, entre otros documentos, el proyecto de carta a Guillermo de Torre (Güiraldes 1962: 30-32); como suele ocurrir en sus documentos privados un ruralismo burlón subraya la idea. Inmediatamente viene una nota precautoria: "Excuso decir que además de esto, y principalmente, es necesario ser un valor independiente de toda sugestión extraña." Así se acuña otro rasgo buscado para su vida mental: fuentes elegidas por vigorosa admiración pero de las que acepta nutrirse en la medida en que no afecten la propia originalidad . . . En una carta algo anterior, sin fecha pero del período mallorquino, como contrapartida a su declarada fidelidad a los maestros franceses manifiesta el tipo de relación que ha establecido con la tradición literaria nacional; lo hace a partir de *Facundo* y de él dice: "No es un libro que me parezca impecable en cuanto a visión, tesis y estilo pero tiene una vida de un raro poder y es tan apasionado que uno a veces creería que está escrito en carne. (. . .) sobre *Facundo* se puede hablar mucho tiempo." Otra invariante, de apreciación, si se confronta con la "Carta europea" de 1925 (Güiraldes 1962: 775), a la vez que ambos testimonios dan razón a las aserciones genéticas sostenidas por Lugones en su famoso artículo sobre *Don Segundo* (1948: 29-44).

En marzo de 1923 comienza a escribirse el "Diario donde toda literatura está ausente", hasta ahora inédito y que hemos estudiado para la *Revista Iberoamericana* (Blasi 1982: 21-29). De él se hablará más adelante. Mientras tanto, una carta, que como todas las que siguen fue escrita en tierra bonaerense, fechada en agosto de 1923, descubre una sutil y normal competencia entablada en la mente del escritor entre el libro que acaba de ser escrito y el que se halla en el telar: *Xaimaca* cuenta, "está en manos del 'imprentero' de San Antonio [de Areco]. Estoy harto de ella. Me aburre como una querida vieja demasiado usada y abusada. (. . .) [*Don Segundo*] no es mejor ni peor. Es otra cosa y Vd. que conoce los primeros capítulos o el primero puede imaginar el estilo del todo." Es normal en la mente de todo escritor cierta tensión o drama interior en el que las *dramatis personae* son los libros a él debidos. Pero en este momento de Güiraldes hay algo más: la lucha contra la sujeción consiguiente a uno que se halla en proceso de textualización y otras obras o actitudes literarias que en esos mismos días se gestan en la mente del escritor; lo dice con simpática llaneza: "Lo que me embroma en todo esto es que mi andar da zancadas, que no pueden seguir mis obras. Las obras que lo tiran a uno dos o tres años para atrás, son una rémora y no he de empezar otra, hasta no contar con el tiempo suficiente para darle fin sin interrupciones. Si estuviese libre hoy, emprendería algo de índole muy diferente." Unos párrafos más abajo explicita las claves de esta lucha secreta: "Recuerda Vd. una conversación que tuvimos en Vichy y en la que algo le dije de una evolución espiritualista? El concepto religioso ha seguido en mí un ascenso. Mi soledad es cada vez más intensa y poblada." El párrafo fecha y consolida lo que se puede ver en sus libros de edición póstuma y lo que se puede inferir y clarificar por la posición numérica y contenido de los dos relatos intercalados en *Don Segundo Sombra* (Blasi 1978: 125-32).

Entre las inéditas al mismo corresponsal, es una de julio de 1924 —dieciséis meses más tarde— la que contiene más rica información: después de *Xaimaca* ha quedado "un tanto exhausto y como perdido en mí mismo. Sería muy largo, muy penoso y tal vez imposible, decirle todo lo que desde entonces ha pasado por mí. No he escrito una palabra, he leído mucho, en cierto sentido [espiritualista?] y me he pasado atento a mi proceso interno, muy confuso y muy atiborrado de episodios. No sé lo que escribiré ahora aunque lo preveo, pero hay cadenas para lo comenzado, y veo mi libertad un poco lejos, más allá de *Don Segundo Sombra*." Curiosa bifurcación: el *homo faber* está labrando pertinazmente su materia sensible mientras su espíritu va ya por otros reinos;

curiosa para la imagen convencional de un artista que está en esos días dando texto a su obra mayor. El resto de la carta, extensa, da noticia de otras situaciones más conocidas: la pertinaz mala salud del escritor que incluiría en aquellos días una depresión, su eterna posición de *outsider* en la escena literaria nacional ("Mi situación, o mejor dicho mi no situación literaria sigue aquí lo mismo.") con mención explícita de desaires inferidos por Lugones, Ricardo Rojas y Horacio Quiroga (Blasi 1983: 140), la malandanza de Xaimaca (sólo 99 ejemplares vendidos a seis meses de su publicación); y también se dan las primeras noticias sobre la constitución del grupo "Proa" al que ya en otros informes hemos estudiado en relación con Güiraldes (Blasi: 1977-1978: 115-127; Blasi 1980: 231-238). La parte pertinente a nuestros propósitos del diario inédito se agota poco después de esta carta y como ya fue dicho de ella se dio razón en la *Revista Iberoamericana*; allí puede leerse cómo Güiraldes entre marzo de 1923 y setiembre del año siguiente cultivaba en su estancia "La Porteña" destrezas de criollo, pintaba y dibujaba, tocaba la guitarra para que su Don Segundo de la realidad bailase las danzas de la tierra, profundizaba su conocimiento del Oriente mientras atendía su maltrecha salud, y mientras *Don Segundo* —aunque no lo escribiera por esos días— gravitaba en el comportamiento del escritor y daba sentido a la totalidad de su conducta, ya que la materia narrada se ponía literalmente a la puerta del cuarto del narrador. Testimonios como éste se repiten: luego de un día de asado, vino y guitarra con un grupo de paisanos dice sabiamente que no ha trabajado en su trabajo de escritor pero que esto no le "mortifica porque de la conversación con los reseros puedo servirme para *Don Segundo Sombra*." No es posible sintetizar la riqueza de ese material más de lo que en aquella revista fue sintetizado; volvamos a las cartas.

El corresponsal francés seguirá recibiendo concreta información sobre el mundo mental de Güiraldes y sobre la construcción de su obra mayor. Esta constituye en su ánimo, junto con la gestión del grupo "Proa", un rechazo de la literatura del *establishment* y de las convenciones vigentes en la institución literaria local, a los que acusa de "decadentes"; así lo dice en diciembre de 1924, con tono de furor contenido, hablando de un joven escritor: "Nada en él de esa lacrimosa debilidad de poeta-sauce que tanto nos sobra: decadentes por falta de propio impulso y que se adjudican una forma de literatura que a un país corresponde por madurez fronteriza del estado senil, creyendo con ello estar en la actitud requerida para el laurel, que ceden las cloróticas falanges de alguna literata romántica de barrio." Esa incriminación de los modos posmodernistas de perduración romántica que afectaban muchos poetas establecidos y su secuela de figuras menores abre un nuevo tema en el contrato literario de Güiraldes con su tiempo, un tema que *in crescendo* llegará a las notas de suelto furor contenidas en la "Carta americana" (Güiraldes 1962: 767-771). Pero para llegar a ella dentro de los límites de intención expresados al comienzo, es preciso pasar por la serie de cartas enviadas por Adelina del Carril, esposa del novelista, al mismo corresponsal francés y amigo de la pareja. Ella cubre con sus cartas la ausencia de otras que debieran haber sido escritas por su marido, en una simpática corresponsalía a dos voces. Los temas que aporta Adelina se alínean con los introducidos hasta aquí por el escritor, enriqueciéndolos a veces de mayor detalle, y siempre de una nueva perspectiva. De ellas hemos dado cuenta en el volumen de homenaje a Güiraldes que editara la Universidad de California con motivo del cincuentenario de su muerte (Blasi 1977: 10-15). Las que nos interesan para nuestros propósitos actuales van de julio de 1925 a agosto del mismo año. Se habla del entusiasmo que los jóvenes escritores tienen por *Don Segundo* y su autor, del "congreso proático perenne que había en casa", de como tal congreso consume el tiempo del novelista, de la recurrente mala salud, de como "los tinterillos de los diarios[con motivo de *Proa*] le tiran a matar a Ricardo con la confabulación del silencio y de la maledicencia", de que Adelina está copiando a máquina el manuscrito de la novela. Y de cómo se ordena el tiempo de escritura sobre el tiempo general del novelista. Luego vienen dos cartas de Güiraldes al mismo corresponsal, fundamentales; se pueden leer en la edición de *Obras completas* (1962: 761-779). Las dos forman un solo cuerpo[2] y de ambas se habla con detenimiento en nuestro *Güiraldes y Larbaud*, el libro que hace una quincena de años dedicamos a los dos corresponsales como protagonista de una amistad ejemplar (Blasi 1970: 61-76). Allí se hace la historia pública y privada de *Proa* con las constancias de su recepción, se insiste en y clarifica el rechazo que el escritor tenía por la ciudad, se documentan los orígenes míticos de *Don Segundo* en la mitología privada de su autor, y finalmente se discute a Hernández y, particularmente, a Sarmiento de manera que amplifica y profundiza lo establecido en la carta de 1920. Algunas de las afirmaciones son capitales para el entendimiento de la poética que rigió la escritura de *Don Segundo*. Como consecuencia de las modificaciones que sus editores le han impuesto, es conveniente trascribir las ideas centrales copiando del documento original. Se dice: "*Facundo* me parece un libro, en partes, de extraño salvajismo y energía, en una modalidad o tono muy distinto del de otros países. ¿Un tono *non-européen*?" Lo pone entre interrogantes, quizás como el oculto testimonio de un inconsciente deseo, de una imagen de la perfección que hubiese querido para la obra que está a punto de concluir. Y aun anticipa los elementos del infortunado juego de palabras con que un Groussac senil dañará más tarde la recepción de *Don Segundo*: "Bajo la levita que el *doctor* ponía sobre el hombre crudo, se me aparece frecuentemente este último (. . .) Recuerde Vd. el tono en que Sarmiento habla del 'baqueano", del 'rastreador' y verá que aunque se propusiera en su acción política destruir al elemento humano autóctono, en el fondo creía profundamente en su ciencia y no sé si exagero suponiendo que sin el pudor de creer en 'supersticiones', Sarmiento enfermo se hubiese puesto en manos de un gaucho que curara con palabras. Esa lucha a brazo partido era en realidad una lucha interior." Este fragmento, muy maltratado en su versión impresa, muestra al vocablo *ciencia* sobresalido y cubriendo todo el campo semántico; ciencia entendida como *gnosis*. La búsqueda de ese saber puede constituir —y creemos constituyó— el sentido último de su *bildungsroman.* Y tal propósito emparenta, se intrinca con las búsquedas espiritualistas que en aquellos mismos días ocupaban la mente del escritor.

Para completar este cuaderno de bitácora es menester regresar a los testimonios provistos por Adelina del Carril. Son cartas de enero a mayo de 1926 (Blasi 1977: 15-19). Hay quejas de que Ricardo "se distrae demasiado en la estancia y trabaja poco", se sabe que ha estado domando una potranca baya de patas negras, y también que en su espíritu "se han producido cambios tan fundamentales que mucho me temo se vaya desinteresando de la literatura. Se acumulan las indicaciones de mala salud y piensa que su obra futura "será completamente distinta de la de ahora". Respecto de *Don Segundo,* añade: "está tan en otra cosa, que lo debe atormentar estar metido en lo que temporalmente le interesa menos, aunque haya sido su pasión más grande, toda su vida." Güiraldes mediante ese *debe* es descripto por su mujer en soledad, en el momento crucial de su escritura; la terrible soledad del poeta que ella no puede ni debe penetrar. Servida de indicios exteriores trata sin embargo de adivinar el paisaje de su alma.[3]

Lo que viene después en las cartas de Adelina, es la jubilosa comunicación del triunfo de *Don Segundo*, de los dos mil ejemplares vendidos en veinte días, de la inmediata edición de cinco mil aún en la imprenta y ya vendida a los libreros, del rumor encomiástico en la ciudad, el éxito de prensa, el artículo consagratorio de Lugones, la inminencia del Premio Nacional. Y luego, las tristes noticias sobre el derrumbe de la salud del novelista. Pero ya estamos fuera del perímetro que nos habíamos propuesto, más allá del libro de bitácora; en pleno tema de la recepción.

En el año centenario de Güiraldes estos datos juntos quizás ayuden a comprender mejor el drama del artista en soledad entregado a su creación y el del productor afanado en su texto mientras la vida de la mente y la de todos los días, como es natural, le tironean en muy diversas y a veces opuestas direcciones. Esa al menos ha sido la intención.

Notas

1 Las cartas inéditas de Ricardo Güiraldes que aquí parcialmente se transcriben, se hallan en su original en el "Fonds Larbaud" de Vichy, bajo la letra *G*; llevan los siguientes números, en orden de transcripción: *604*, París 6 diciembre 1919; *605*, París 4 enero 1920; *607*, Puerto Pollensa (Mallorca) 31 marzo 1920; *611*, París 4 julio 1920; *615*, Mallorca 1920; *620*, estancia "La Porteña" (provincia de Buenos Aires) 19 agosto 1923; *622*, Buenos Aires 5 julio 1924; *623*, "La Porteña" 1 diciembre 1924.

2 La primera de ellas, "Carta americana", fue recibida por Valery Larbaud sin indicación de lugar y fecha. La segunda, "Carta europea", es del 15 de octubre de 1925, tampoco lleva indicación de lugar. En su versión impresa fueron introducidas fechas erradas así como modificaciones de detalle en el texto que en ciertos casos alteran el sentido de algunas frases. En el "Fonds Larbaud" llevan respectivamente las signaturas *G 624* y *G 625*.

3 Según Adelina tenían en proyecto un viaje a la India, una vez que *Don Segundo* estuviese publicado.

Bibliografía

Blasi, Alberto

1970 *Güiraldes y Larbaud: Una amistad creadora.* Buenos Aires.

1977 "Las cartas de Adelina del Carril". In William E. Megenney (ed.): *Four Essays on Ricardo Güiraldes*, pp. 1-37, Riverside: University of California.

1977 a "La ruta de Don Segundo". *Chasqui*, 6: 7-14. Swarthmore (Pennsylvania).

1978 "Mito y escritura en *Don Segundo Sombra*". *Revista Iberoamericana*, 44: 125-32. Pittsburgh.

1978 a "Ricardo Güiraldes y *Proa*". *Boletín de la Academia Norteamericana de la Lengua Española*, 2-3: 115-27. New York.

1980 "Contribuciones ensayísticas de Güiraldes". *Los ensayistas*, 8-9: 141-145. Athens (Georgia).

1981 "Revaluación del martinfierrismo". En Giuseppe Bellini (ed.): *Actas del séptimo congreso de la Asociación Internacional de Hispanistas*, Roma.

1982 "Vanguardismo en el Río de la Plata: Un 'diario' y una *Exposición*". *Revista Iberoamericana*, 48: 21-36. Pittsburgh.

1983 "Estudio preliminar y cronología". En Ricardo Güiraldes: *Don Segundo Sombra. Prosas y poemas*, pp. 131-155, 303-312. Caracas.

Güiraldes, Ricardo

1962 *Obras completas*. Buenos Aires.

Lugones, Leopoldo

1948 "*Don Segundo Sombra* de Ricardo Güiraldes". En Ricardo Güiraldes: *Don Segundo Sombra*, pp. 29-44, Madrid.

Ocampo, Victoria

1941 *Testimonios*. Buenos Aires.

RAYUELA: LA IMAGINACION COMO METAFORA

Pedro Cuperman
Syracuse University

a N. Rodríguez Bustamante

En el primer capítulo de la segunda lectura posible de *Rayuela,** Morelli habla de un napolitano que se "pasó años sentado a la puerta de su casa mirando un tornillo en el suelo. Por la noche lo untaba y lo ponía debajo del colchón. El tornillo fue primero risa, tomada de pelo, irritación comunal, junta de vecinos, signo de violación de los deberes cívicos, finalmente encogimiento de hombros, la paz, el tornillo fue la paz, nadie podía pasar por la calle sin mirar de reojo el tornillo y sentir que era la paz. El tipo murió de un síncope, y el tornillo desapareció ni bien acudieron los vecinos. Uno de ellos lo guarda, quizá lo saca en secreto y lo mira, vuelve a sacarlo y se va a la fábrica sintiendo algo que no comprende, una oscura reprobación. Sólo se calma cuando saca el tornillo y lo mira, se queda mirándolo hasta que oye pasos y lo guarda presuroso."

Veinte años después, Sudamericana reabre esta "caja de Pandora" y nos ofrece, precedido por un estudio crítico de Ana María Barrenechea, *El Cuaderno de Bitácora de "Rayuela"*.[1] Están ahí el relato La Araña,[2] la escena de Talita en el tablón, (escenas nucleares las llama Cortázar) la de los hilos, y también el orden narrativo Buenos Aires-París, que luego se invierte, acompañado por reflexiones sobre la novela, diagnósticos sobre la personalidad argentina, y el orientalismo de Cortázar (en traducciones de Mircea Eliade, sin duda, pero también en lecturas del orientalista Vicente Fatone, su maestro en la Escuela Normal Mariano Acosta).[3] Es inútil enumerar la lista de pre/textos que, por otra parte, forman el excelente estudio de Barrenechea. Todo, invención, estructura, lenguaje, se tiende hacia *Rayuela.*

Releída desde el Cuaderno, *Rayuela* significa novela del proceso de la imaginación, y lo que indica la nueva lectura es que lo imaginado por el Cuaderno no se traduce; *Rayuela* no es un texto inducido, representado; se convierte según la técnica del revelado y la ampliación: y ese modelo de la creatividad será el espejo en que se nutre.

EL PRE-TEXTO

El tema del pre/texto como puente para otro texto debe ser incluído en el análisis de *Rayuela*. Es casi una revelación releer *Rayuela* a la luz del *Cuaderno* sabiendo que son textos entrelazados, que los mitos y símbolos y las figuras de uno son en verdad metáforas para que surjan los mitos, los símbolos, las figuras del otro. A diferencia de otras novelísticas, no se trataría tanto del marco semiótico del espacio de la obra como de su grado de totalización. El pre/texto forma parte de aquellos modos de producción de realización mediata: en el caso del arquitecto, el proyecto imaginario tiende a borrarse a medida que el proyecto real se concreta. Pero aun así, el proyecto no se desvanece frente a la obra. Es más, se trata de una operación que preserva todos y cada uno de los trazos del trabajo: el momento de la *inventio* contiene la *dispositio*, y el encuentro se resuelve en *elocutio*. Para el literato, para el estudiante de retórica que quiere vencer "el terror inicial a la página en blanco" y escribir, cada una de las etapas propedéuticas —leer, copiar, inventar, clasificar, organizar secuencias, y finalmente la escritura— es una acumulación sucesiva, y cada sucesión se resuelve en otra cosa.

Podría decirse que la existencia del *Cuaderno*, permite tratar la discusión de *Rayuela* como un ejemplo emblemático del diálogo proyecto-obra que, en mi opinión, debe fundarse no tanto en la explicable debilidad de los proyectos en relación a la obra concluída, y publicada, como en la presencia virtual, latente de una *Tejne* (arte y artificio para Aristóteles) en el centro mismo de la imaginación artística. De nada ayuda llamarlo cuasi-ficción. ¿No es acaso privilegio del autor decidir qué es ficción? ¿No es la sociedad, la historia, la época, quienes deciden cómo se ha de leer un texto?

Max Black veía afinidad entre el modelo y la metáfora. Si en poesía metáfora designa un signo de lo imaginario, en ciencia modelo denota un instrumento heurístico, cuya lógica tiene sus fuentes en la imaginación. Entre razón e imaginación se interponen no tanto realidades como modos de acceso.[4] Para lo imaginario —Black habla de modelos teóricos— inventar y descubrir no son opciones sino operaciones coexistentes. El *Cuaderno*, leído desde *Rayuela*, es este modo de acceso del que habla Black: una operación de lo imaginario que inventa, descubre, dispone, pero a veces se posesiona y escribe.

El *Cuaderno* es un pre/texto para nosotros, no porque haya algo esencial que así lo determine sino porque en primer lugar lo fue para Cortázar. Y lo fue como una condición operativa de alguien que no se sintió obligado a pensar la totalidad sino a ir resolviendo su creatividad sectorialmente. En sus tensiones y trazos se anuncia lo que confirma la estructura, se anuncia *Rayuela.*

Los estudios del pre/texto sólo fragmentariamente registran esta ambigüedad del pasaje del proyecto a la obra. Las determinaciones de antemano no bastan para saber qué es texto y qué pre-texto. En relación a la novela, el lenguaje del diario es metalenguaje. *El Cuaderno de Bitácora de "Rayuela"* es ese registro, y también refugio de una inminencia entrópica en el umbral de su realización. Casi siempre el diario rehuye la ambigüedad. Bastaría abrir al azar el *Cuaderno* para descubrir que ahí se anuncia el lenguaje de *Rayuela*, que ahí comienzan las *correspondencias*—y pienso en Baudelaire—que luego han de reiterar ciudades y personajes, lecturas posibles y "deslecturas". Desde el *Cuaderno* se entienden las búsquedas de *Rayuela*: encontrar una retórica que dé cuenta del deseo sin exorcizarlo, y no ya en la historia ni en las cosas sino en la sede misma del deseo: la palabra. "Aimez bien, vigoureusement, crânement, orientalement, férocement, celle que vous aimez . . . " había escrito Baudelaire. Los mismos motivos simbolistas y decadentes de Bestiario, en *Rayuela* adquieren una suerte de humanidad que acaba mordiéndose la cola.

En *Rayuela*, y en el *Cuaderno*, la pregunta por el Yo converge en la pregunta por la imaginación. De esa modalidad surge el carácter subjuntivo, interrogativo de una literatura del discurso cauteloso. Por algo proliferan las citas, la des/construcción narrativa y por algo Cortázar se vale, entre otras cosas, de la voz mediadora de Morelli. Pero el Yo de la narración está poseído, sumergido en el lenguaje. No es la pura disponibilidad enfrentada a la pura plenitud de lo real. "Me estoy atando los zapatos, contento, silbando, y de pronto la infelicidad. Pero esta vez te pesqué, angustia, te sentí *previa* a cualquier organización mental, al primer juicio de negación" (p. 426). Cortázar ni era un filósofo ni se proponía escribir una novela filosófica. Comienza a redactar el *Cuaderno* en París, cuando la filosofía dominante es el existencialismo de Sartre. Bastaría reflexionar en las reflexiones de Morelli para confirmar que su escepticismo literario no es negatividad, no se contagia a la escritura (es decir, al swing donde nace y crece la escritura (capítulo 82). Aun en los momentos de mayor duda y melancolía, Morelli rechaza la anterioridad de la Nada. Cortázar no se deja tentar por la voluntad constructiva de hacer del Yo pura posibilidad, pura indeterminación, y del mundo plena completud, presencia masiva (las "construcciones" categoriales de *El Ser y la Nada*).[5] En *Rayuela,* en vez de La Nada, el Vacío, en vez de la oposición posible-imposible, la escritura registro de sí misma, y a través de ésta, lectura del mundo.

Por momentos se tiene la impresión de que entre Oliveira y la Maga encarnan dos visiones dicotómicas del origen: el origen en el pasado y el origen en el instante. Sería inútil enumerar la larga lista de rasgos semánticos que definen estas dicotomías. Todo, personajes, narrativa, el lenguaje y los espacios parecerían ajustarse a las novelas de la pérdida y la recuperación (quizá haya que mencionar que la doble pérdida de La Maga, en el capítulo 1 y el 29, tras la muerte de Rocamadour, hace pensar en las reflexiones Lacanianas acerca del mito de Eurídice). Sin duda en la biblioteca mental de Cortázar están Proust y también Breton, Buñuel, Dalí, Max Ernst: los surrealistas. Pero nada más lejano del Cortázar del *Cuaderno* y de *Rayuela* que la idea de una anterioridad esencial o de un Yo prisionero del lenguaje. Tanto el narrador de *A la recherche du temps perdu* como el de *Nadja* siguen movidos, fundados por el *cógito* cartesiano. Uno se busca en contingencias involuntarias, el otro minando la cárcel verbal que lo aprisiona, pero ambos viven como opción última cancelar la distancia del Yo, recobrarlo y recobrarse. Ninguna de las pesadillas de *Rayuela* se inicia o concluye con esa esperanza.

EL ORDEN DE LO FANTASTICO

En el Río de la Plata se practicó con asiduidad lo fantástico: Quiroga, Macedonio, Borges—para citar el caso emblemático—, todos leyeron a Poe, todos exploraron la frontera semiótica del texto que con tanta asiduidad atravesaba Poe. Borges, en *Las ruinas circulares*, imagina un proyecto donde la imaginación y lo real (el sueño) se contaminan y ocurre esa superimposición ontológica, la famosa *lecture en abîme.* El mismo procedimiento en Cortázar aparece siempre como apetencia de sustancia. Optica doble, estereofonía aún ante la muerte. En *La noche boca arriba* no importa tanto saber cuál de los mundos del personaje es la realidad y cuál el sueño, sino si al despertar—en la vida o en la muerte—sobrevivirán la mariposa y la crisálida. En *Rayuela*, como observa Ana María Barrenechea, las exigencias del "género novela—en oposición al género cuento—tal como Cortázar lo imaginaba entonces, no le permitía ese tipo de libertades con el nivel de lo narrado, ni la ruptura total de las convenciones de *normalidad/anormalidad* que han elaborado los códigos culturales y nuestra experiencia de la naturaleza".[6] Pero quizá no sea fortuito agregar que ya desde el comienzo ese mundo lo ocupan seres sitiados por las coordenadas del modelo Occidental y que precisamente es ese eje de coordenadas lo que denuncia y des/construyen las metáforas, la estructura, la exacerbación del allá y del acá, del comienzo, del descenso, y la concomitante separación entre *creatura* y *cosmos.*

Ana María Barrenechea cuestiona el orientalismo de Cortázar. Advierte que tras aludir por boca de Morelli a la mística y a las filosofías de la India, Cortázar las descarta porque "si bien aspiran a elevadas superaciones de las dicotomías occidentales, lo hacen con marcado carácter individualista."[7] Lo novedoso de *Rayuela* consistió en meditar esos conceptos sin teorizarlos o, para usar una palabra de Lacan, teorizando su *meconnaisance:* " . . . —Wong se aprovechó más tarde para edificar una complicada teoría sobre las saturaciones sexuales; según él se podría avanzar en el conocimiento siempre que en un momento dado se lograra un coeficiente tal de amor (son sus palabras, usted perdone la jerga china) que el espíritu cristalizara bruscamente en otro plano, se instalara en una surrealidad. ¿Usted cree, Lucía?" (p. 163)

Cortázar recorta del Zen la estética que superpone espacio y tiempo pero en *Rayuela* se resiste a traducirlos en relato o en categorías constructivas de lo imaginario. En una de sus últimas entrevistas subraya la impresión que siempre le causaron esos tópicos. Y al referirse a una escena de *Paradiso*, de Lezama Lima, no titubea en aludir al Zen y a lo maravilloso y en hacerlo en referencia a su propia actitud ante la escritura:

> . . . el personaje, creo que es José Semí, ve en la vitrina de un anticuario una serie de objetos de jade, de cristal. Y de golpe se da cuenta de que esas cosas, que componen una figura, no son objetos separados sino una especie de conjunto, que se están influyendo mutuamente.[8]

Lo maravilloso, las figuras, estos conceptos que en apariencia son el metalenguaje de la crítica, en Cortázar tienen el valor de una ontología propia, basada en la experiencia personal.[9]

Lo que distingue a *Rayuela* de otras novelas, sobre todo de los últimos años de novela en Latinoamérica, es la estrecha relación entre el texto y su *inventio* y *dispositio,* génesis inseparable de las múltiples lecturas, y por lo tanto de su estructura. Ya antes de la publicación del *Cuaderno* sabíamos que iba a llamarse *Mandala,* nombre que acentúa el *Origen* sin origen, signo topológico y sobre todo itinerario de las ruminaciones meditativas del texto. Novelas como *Cien años de sole-*

dad, por ejemplo, acentúan el carácter totalizador de sus coordenadas temporales, de ahí que al hablar de tiempo cíclico haya que referirse a la precedencia de la lógica narrativa sobre la escritura. *Rayuela* no conoce otro tiempo que el de sus tránsitos. El *Cuaderno* al principio concibe el movimiento en forma centrífuga—la escena del tablón en Buenos Aires precede a las escenas de París, envían a París; pero a la mitad de camino el *Cuaderno* registra su reverso a lo que será la versión definitiva: Paris-Buenos Aires, el retorno al agujero en el circo, al manicomio, al origen centrípeto de donde nacen y donde se bifurcan las *figuras.* Lo que se gestaba como proyecto hacia afuera—el exilio—a través de una espléndida cartografía de fracasos acabó en la versión definitiva del retorno. Un trayecto que va de la historia amorosa de Oliveira y La Maga a la historia azarosa de la búsqueda y a la culminación argentina en el manicomio, y al fin, o en el medio, la bibliografía mental de Cortázar a la hora de escribir *Rayuela:* los "capítulos prescindibles".

La Rayuela en el fondo de un traspatio de Buenos Aires, el tablón en el vacío, los hilos, el puente, el agujero en la carpa del circo son mitos, en el sentido de Barthes, de la novela y de la vida azarosa de sus personajes. Oliveira y la Maga, Traveler y Talita, Morelli, todos lo saben, puesto que nacieron excesivamente personajes, excesivamente conscientes. La semiosis que inician bien podría reeditar la lectura perspectivista (pienso en El cuarteto de Alejandría, de Lawrence Durrell), de no intervenir esa conversión metafórica que Cortázar llama *Figuras* y que habría que pensar como un ejercicio, un *como si* no ya kantiano sino iniciático. Lo provisorio de una poética reticente, en el sentido que le da Lezama Lima cuando dice que Cortázar prefiere lo efímero y lo gratuito, el goce: la *Paideuma*, al culto del crescendo de los Wagnerianos.[10] Reticente, porque como en el caso de escritores como Sterne o Macedonio, aquello que otros consideran la Obra en ellos es tan sólo tentativa de aproximación: la imaginación como proyecto (la antípoda sería el caso de Borges, el proyecto como imaginación).

El tema de lo imaginario, así figurado, acaba en una arquitectura que no se totaliza. Del origen ausente—el relato La Araña—a la escena de Talita en el tablón ("al filo de la navaja" dicen los monjes del Budismo), a la guerra de los hilos todo se divide y se divierte. Mientras más se metaforizan las relaciones topológicas, mientras aumentan la expectativa y los espejismos y más disponible queda el campo de la imaginación y más jactancioso y lúcido el texto, más risible y más efímera se vuelve la transcendencia. Eventos, personajes, escritura—todo del *Cuaderno* a *Rayuela*—apunta a ese doble horizonte.

En el capítulo 73, el primero de la segunda lectura de *Rayuela*, "Morelli pensaba que el tornillo debía ser otra cosa, . . . pero también que a lo mejor el Napolitano era un idiota, y aun así pudo ser el inventor de un mundo. Del tornillo a un ojo, de un ojo a una estrella . . . ¿Por qué entregarse a la Gran Costumbre?"

Entre el pre/texto y el texto, entre los núcleos seminales y la obra, entre los intertextos, su reescritura y la duplicación de metáforas: París-Buenos Aires, el relato lineal y el desplazado, emerge una poética de la creatividad. De la creatividad que la busca. En *Rayuela*, aun antes de la publicación del *Cuaderno*, lo que regía no eran los temas o símbolos sino el tema de los símbolos, su inclusión azarosa en la imaginación, y la posibilidad de que todo ello concretara en texto.

Azarosos como en *Nadja* son los encuentros de Oliveira y la Maga, imprevisibles como las alquimias verbales de Rimbaud son las metáforas, figurativa en el sentido tropológico de la búsqueda es la narratividad. Azar, alquimia, inconsciente. Sin duda fueron y son estos estandartes del surrealismo, pero el Yo de Bretón es todavía el Yo anterior del *cógito*, y el de *Rayuela* un resultado de la imaginación: "Paraíso perdido, perdido por buscarte."

De la lectura conjunta del pre-texto y el texto en mutua proyección surge la *Tejne* de una escritura donde convergen la poética y la ontología del origen de la escritura.

Entre ambas parecerían inscribirse los versos del RigVeda: "¿Quién, pues, lo sabe? ¿Quién ha declarado el origen de esta creación? Los dioses vienen después, entonces, ¿quién sabe de dónde ha surgido? Aquel que dio lugar a la creación, la haya o no creado el mismo, el más vidente en el más alto de los cielos. Ese quizá lo sepa. ¿O quizá ni él lo sabe?"

Notas

* Julio Cortázar, *Rayuela* (Buenos Aires: Editorial Sudamericana, 1975), Décimo-octava edición. Todas las citas remiten a la presente edición.

1 Julio Cortázar, Ana María Barrenechea, *Cuaderno de Bitácora de Rayuela*, (Bs. As.: Sudamericana, 1983).

2 Publicada por primera vez en *Revista Iberoamericana*, 84-85 (julio-diciembre de 1973) 388-398.

3 Para la relación de Cortázar con Fatone véase O. Prego, *La Fascinación de las Palabras,* (Bs. As.: Muchnik Editores, 1985), p. 30.

4 Max Black, *Models and Metaphors,* (Ithaca: Cornell Univ. Press, 1962).

[5] "It is not experience of the thing and of the world precisely the ground that we need in order to think nothingness in any way whatever?" M. Merleau-Ponty, *The Visible and the Invisible* (Evanston: Northwestern University Press, 1968) p. 148-49. Según Barrenechea, Cortázar estaría emparentado con el Existencialismo Sartreano pero difieren en "lo fundamental, que es la busca trascendente de Horacio . . . en efecto, el protagonista vivió siempre desarraigado y excentrado en París igual que en Buenos Aires, aún antes de partir. Su mutilación es una negatividad consciente practicada como instrumento para alcanzar la plenitud, romper las trabas espacio-temporales y librarse de la condición humana de la elección." Barrenechea, p. 116-117.

[6] Barrenechea, p. 41.

[7] "No me puedo salvar solo. No me puedo salvar sin que se salven los otros." (*Rayuela* 491) citado por Barrenechea, p. 59. Quizá el problema no es tanto del misticismo ni de la India sino el de algunas de sus escuelas filosóficas. Como se sabe, en la India Budista bajo el emperador Asoka (siglo III) se desarrolló la corriente llamada del Gran Vehículo, el *MahaYana*, precisamente, un mesianismo de orden colectivo. Entre el ascético individualismo Brahmánico y el helenizante colectivismo de Asoka, surge la mediadora figura del *Bodhisattva*: el santo inconcluso, que habiendo alcanzado la liberación se detiene en el umbral del Nirvana para interceder en la salvación de otros seres. Según Fatone: "implica la posibilidad de que la retribución que un hombre hubiera debido recibir por sus acciones pasadas sea transferida voluntariamente a otros para ayudarlos en el camino de la salvación. V. Fatone, "El Budhismo Nihilista" en *Obras Completas* (Bs. As.: Sudamericana, 1972), Vol. II.

[8] Prego, p. 118.

[9] "Sí, eso forma parte de esa intuición de lo que yo llamo las figuras. Es decir, el hecho de que elementos que para las leyes naturales no están relacionados o no son heterogéneos—como puede ser este radiador, esta mesa, aquel teléfono—en determinados procesos de intuición (e incluso de distracción, como se dan en la filosofía Zen) se enlazan instantáneamente, crean una especie de figura que no tiene por que ser de tipo material. Puede producirse a partir de ideas, sentimientos, colores." Op. Cit.

[10] "Cortázar por Lezama Lima", *Jaque*, (Montevideo, 17 de Feb. de 1984), p. 7.

EXPERIENCIA EXILICA Y PROCESO CREATIVO EN LA LITERATURA ARGENTINA CONTEMPORANEA

Ludmila Kapschutschenko
Rider College

El exilio es una constante de la realidad diaria de Latinoamérica. El creciente fenómeno envuelve a gente de diversos países, clases y edades por razones sociales, económicas y políticas. Gabriel García Márquez se refiere al mismo en su discurso de aceptación del Premio Nobel de Literatura en 1982, explicando los variados aspectos. En sus textos más recientes, Julio Cortázar ha destacado los valores que pueden resultar de la literatura del exilio, afirmando: " . . . sé que cuando llegue la hora de que los críticos y los especialistas tracen el panorama de la literatura latinoamericana de nuestros días, la creación nacida en el exilio será un capítulo con características propias pero en plena ligazón con toda nuestra entera realidad . . . nos hará adelantar hacia nuestra identidad profunda . . . que nos mostrará por fin nuestro destino histórico como continente."[1]

En la última década, la Argentina ha vivido en un período de censura oficial y autocensura cuyas consecuencias se han convertido en los temas más recurrentes en los escritos de los que han sufrido exilio; estudios políticos, psicológicos y sociológicos han invadido la escena cultural tratando de explicar el por qué y el cómo de todo lo ocurrido. En *El exilio es el nuestro* (1986), Carlos A. Brocato se refiere al exilio interno y externo—de los "quedados" e "idos"—, preguntándose si los que vivieron en otras realidades enriquecieron su óptica de la vida social; opina que en la producción del exilio exterior no hay exámenes orgánicos ni aportes parciales que hayan contribuido a que los argentinos se conozcan "más a fondo".[2] Un análisis literario puede ofrecer respuesta. En el presente estudio propongo tener en cuenta las observaciones citadas y tratar de establecer su aplicación a las obras de tres autores argentinos que escribieron fuera de su país: Humberto Costantini, Mempo Giardinelli y Juan Carlos Martini. Sus últimas creaciones permiten un enfoque literario del exilio, con muestras similares pero a la vez distintas de reacciones a la experiencia exílica. Se estudiarán en un orden que permite notar mejor las diferencias.

En *La larga noche de Francisco Sanctis* (1984), Costantini ya había presentado al hombre común porteño, cercado por el terror. Los avances y retrocesos mentales ante la exigencia de actuar, vaivenes entre el egoísmo y la solidaridad en un estado de represión también surgen en la obra titulada *En la noche* (1985), de cinco cuentos y tres poemas, cuyo título metafórico designa los oscuros años bajo la dictadura militar reciente en que reinaron el terror y la muerte. Con tono callejero, y empleo abundante del lunfardo, que sirve como modo expresivo y forma de sentir, el autor presenta situaciones irremediables que comienzan como anécdotas inocentes para luego inscribirse en caminos de progresiva desesperación por parte de los protagonistas, y de creciente tensión para el lector.

El miedo y el exilio no deseado sirven como base temática principal; el primero es parte de la cotidianeidad, observado por diferentes perspectivas de los personajes; el segundo conlleva el imperativo de reafirmar en tierra extraña la personalidad porteña, el ser argentino. Muchos personajes, complejos psicológicamente, existieron realmente (indicándose esto en notas y dedicatorias). Encuadrados dentro de cánones realistas, hechos verídicos son transformados por la subjetividad del proceso creativo que otorga vitalidad, i.e.: en "Noticia", poema escrito a raíz de una crónica periodística, donde se informa escuetamente del asesinato de dos abogadas defensoras de presos políticos, el autor intercala trozos del periódico vitalizándolos con su interpretación y suplemento a lo no dicho. Integrándose a la intriga como un personaje más nos acerca al génesis del hecho literario: en el relato "Guardado" cuenta sobre un manuscrito comprometido hallado por su familia en 1979 y remitido a él; narrando un caso político real confiesa las dificultades de convertirlo en ficción. El poema "Tango" es un episodio real autobiográfico sobre la relación con una "gringa" en México que quiere infundirle el gusto por la vida mientras él quiere sufrir sin interrupciones por el país lejano, ya que "porteñamente hipocondríaco, tangueramente triste" quiere "añorar hasta la última gota de sangre el terruño natal."[3]

En "Cacería sangrienta o la daga de Pat Sullivan", el protagonista nos cuenta de sus creaciones para la Serie Negra, Colección Terror o la Super Crimen en México, escribiendo bajo diferentes seudónimos, y creando personajes como Pat Sullivan que ejemplifican la violencia. Dos jóvenes argentinos le relatan los verdaderos hechos sufridos en carne propia; mientras describen detalles de las torturas, él sólo piensa en cómo adaptar lo contado a sus propias historias ficticias. Al final se pregunta "cómo cocinar todo ese material sin mayor significación artística" . . . "porque, ojo, no es cuestión de sacar una fotocopia de los hechos (despelotes en la Argentina, repre parapolicial, tortura, etc.) . . . Es cuestión de tomar lo que . . . contaron . . . pero agregándole detalles de suspenso, dramatismo . . .como para que el lector se meta en el asunto" (21). Los jóvenes le agradecen que intelectuales como él, "comprometidos" con el pueblo, difundan "las cosas que pasan allá en el país". Al oír esto, sabiéndose un oportunista, se emborracha y tiene ganas de pegarse un tiro por remordimiento. El relato "En la noche" muestra a un hombre que vuelve a su casa sólo para ser atrapado por los parapoliciales desde sus coches Ford Falcon; ruega que sea un sueño y se despierta; "Tal vez esta semana llegue una carta de ellos, se dice (sin pronunciar tampoco ahora el nombre de sus hijos), el humo del cigarrillo asciende lentamente hacia el techo encalado de una piecita de Colonia Anzures, en México, a nueve mil kilómetros de Buenos Aires" (85)—con este abrupto final nos enteramos que se trata de un exiliado y sus pesadillas. En "La promesa" vemos cómo coinciden en el mismo individuo un ser con facetas humanas y un torturador: una madre visita a Raúl, ahora policía, para pedirle que salve a Oscar, antiguo compañero de juegos; por temor a perder su carrera, no quiere comprometerse y cuando le tienta la idea de sentirse "un muchacho de buen corazón" ya es tarde—Oscar ha muerto torturado.

No siempre las imágenes recordadas le permiten escribir. El poema "Rosedal" centra el lugar idealizado en un parque porteño en su "odiamada" Argentina; tratando de escapar con la imaginación y la literatura de "ese despelotudo y en cierto modo pelotudo cangrejal del exilio" (177), quiere "ingresar más o menos clandestinamente en su país/ . . . recuperar sin demasiado riesgo/ una patria lejana/ a la que ya estaba francamente podrido/ de imaginar de saber bañada en sangre/ infestada de fachos y milicos/ enferma perseguida robada picaneada/ atravesado su aire/ no por lánguidos lamentos de acordeones/ sino por los terribles gritos de los torturados" (180). Cada vez que crea escenas bellas se le aparece un "automóvil Ford Falcon negro"; trata de "eliminarlo . . ./ de su imaginación y de su vista y del papel" (203) pero a la tercera vez que se le apareció entonces "arrancó de un tirón la hoja del rodillo/ y el rodillo hizo un ruidito agudo sibilante/ como de sierra o de quejido/ y la deseada historia quedó así/ para siempre inconclusa" (204)—así concluye el libro.

En "Guardado", cuando al autor le tocaría describir una tortura, se detiene y reflexiona diciendo que es imposible describir con un mínimo de verdad la tortura desde el punto de vista del torturado o "meterse en la piel de quien está sometido a ese dolor, y padecerlo con él" (129-30). El dolor como exiliado sí lo puede expresar, pero con vacíos cada vez que los monstruos se ciernen sobre él. No se da por vencido en sus intentos porque le guían sentimientos de temor y culpa debidos a "la imposibilidad de proteger a . . . seres queridos en aquella Argentina saqueada y asesinada" (147). Escribe porque necesita "expulsar" sus historias "para siempre de sí", éstas rondan como fantasmas y debe ahuyentarlas. Confiesa: "Algunos suelen llamar a esto exorcismo" (148).

Mempo Giardinelli en *La revolución en bicicleta* (1980) habló de exiliados del extranjero viviendo en Argentina. En *El cielo con las manos* (1981) un exiliado argentino relata su historia a un tal don Jaime, descrito solamente como "una especie de gran oreja omnicomprensiva",[4] o sea el lector-oyente. El narrador-protagonista cuenta cómo a los trece años se enamora de Aurora, la espía en el baño por el ojo de la cerradura, la extraña y recuerda hasta que veinte años más tarde la encuentra casualmente en México; este último hecho desencadena la serie de tumultuosas imágenes del pasado que llevan su memoria al ambiente de su juventud en el Chaco y luego en Buenos Aires. Con el encuentro se enfrenta al pasado y al presente; las fantasías eróticas de antes, al unirse él a ella sexualmente ahora, ceden paso a un desencanto que implica la madurez. Lo que antes le hacía tocar "el cielo con las manos" ahora le hace "tocar la tierra con los pies" (171). En una visión divertida y trágica tenemos la historia del paraíso perdido, recobrado y desechado definitivamente. Los vaivenes de la nostalgia que llevan al narrador del presente en México al pasado en Argentina, de un modo fragmentado, como lo regula la memoria, nos pintan cuadros vívidos, tiernos y tristes de la vida en los dos países. Los lenguajes de ambos también se entremezclan dando lugar a un estilo de giros acuñado en la novela como "argenmex" (75). Noticias, olores, ruidos provocan nostalgia: "y me sentí desesperar, no sabía dónde estaba, si en Resistencia hace veinte años, o si en México, ahora, la semana pasada" (26). Cuenta: "Iba caminando por Reforma cuando de pronto me pareció escuchar el canto de una cigarra. . . . Y qué solo estaba. . . . todo porque me faltaba una cigarra chaqueña" (47).

Los recuerdos traen fantasmas; Costantini los quiere expulsar, Giardinelli los necesita: "Uno no puede vivir sin fantasmas" (55), dice; quiere convivir con los recuerdos, repensar la vida, detener el tiempo; se aferra al pasado porque es el único que se tiene (120). Aurora, con su presencia, es el recuerdo encarnado y como tal produce pánico porque hay que encararlo frente a frente: "Quizá el tembladeral empieza con el solo hecho de no tener patria, de haberla perdido" (108), explica. Se refiere también a su generación: "Somos jóvenes todavía, y sin embargo aquí nos tienen, desperdigados por el mundo como si proviniéramos de un hormiguero al que alguien pateó. . . . salimos para impregnar de nostalgia todo, sobre cualquier tierra" (75). Se considera parte de una generación "perdida". La culpa surge al pensar en los propios hijos nacidos en el exilio que asumen "una nostalgia impropia", que se contagian de las añoranzas por partida doble, y que tal vez les juzguen por imponerles un "desarraigo prematuro" (108). Las palabras "son el único recurso que se tiene para llenar el vacío" (129). El tiempo, la distancia y el dolor son "inenarrables" pero el tratar de "verbalizarlos" ayuda. Y hay necesidad de quedar "aferrado a una oreja"—a un lector, para que el amor y el odio, producidos en este caso por el exilio, "duelan menos".

La novela *Qué solos se quedan los muertos* (1985) es, según el autor, un homenaje a México, una rendición de cuentas en el sentido de incorporar cierta mexicanidad en la prosa. El exilio es una paradoja, un doble juego patético ya que es una pérdida y una ganancia: se coexiste con dos geografías, dos historias, dos estilos de vida. El distanciamiento permite "repensar y reflexionar sobre la propia sociedad; el autocuestionamiento, la revisión crítica del pasado son esenciales para el posible reencuentro y recuperación de lo perdido".[5] Para esta obra elige la forma narrativa policial, adecuada al caso, ya que por definición la novela negra funciona "como un ejercicio de investigación de la conducta social y de concienciación crítica".[6] Hay en ella violencia, intento de elucidación de enigmas, restablecimiento precario de la verdad.[7]

El autor explica que "este texto . . . no es ni pretende ser una novela policial"[8] para que intuyamos su otro nivel—el de la reflexión sobre la década del '70 vivida en el país. La acción transcurre en Zacatecas, ciudad mexicana. José Giustozzi, periodista argentino, es llamado por Hilda, amiga de su ex novia Carmen, también exiliada. Encuentra a Carmen cambiada y apenada por el asesinato de un compañero argentino. Al poco tiempo ella muere misteriosamente; él decide descubrir la verdad. Mientras recorre la ciudad reflexiona sobre el pasado personal, el vivido con Carmen durante los comienzos del '70 cuando regresaba Perón y la violencia crecía. En actitud crítica, mientras vive una extraña realidad donde los cadáveres son hechos concretos, trata de encontrar las causas profundas que llevaron a su generación al enfrentamiento y la muerte. Al querer enfrentarse con el enigma de la muerte de la mujer amada, se convierte de espectador en actor; sólo alcanza a ser un "antihéroe" que quiere ir más allá de sus limitaciones.

Relatando en primera persona, dirigiéndose a "alguien" que "alguna vez" lea el texto, explica que lo escrito "ha sido una manera de descargar tensiones, de desahogar(se)", es un "testimonio apresurado . . . también desesperado" (218). Como en la otra novela, la mujer lo lleva a un pasado—esta vez indescifrable. La nostalgia surge por asociaciones visuales y auditivas—el alarido al estilo mariachi le recuerda a los sapukays de su tierra chaqueña (notemos que para Giardinelli el exilio es múltiple pues su provincia y ciudad nativas son fundamentales para su identidad); se agrega además un mencionado abandono por parte de los padres que añade a la sensación de orfandad por triple partida. Aurora antes y ahora Carmen representan el amor que, según el narrador, es "la única metáfora de Dios" (100)—con ellas desaparece esa metáfora que ayuda a sobrevivir. Al meditar sobre los años que habían arruinado al país mucho antes de los '70, y al no encontrar respuestas ni saber por qué tenía que encontrarlas, se consuela diciendo: "lo terrible en todo caso es quedarse fuera de la historia, sin brújula y sin destino, como sólo quedan los muertos" (134). La pregunta sobre la posible salvación del hombre queda sin respuesta; se nos dice que quizá esté "en la dignidad con que se recorre el propio camino" . . . porque el hombre "finalmente, no es más que la metáfora de sus acciones, una metáfora erratil y confusa que nadie, nunca, explicará realmente" (196)—con dichas observaciones universaliza su obra.

La idea del hombre en busca de sí mismo surge también en las obras de Juan Carlos Martini. El mismo aclara que la distancia del exilio afectó su escritura pues comprendió que se había desplazado físicamente de los ejes de la historia argentina. Así intuyó la idea de "una escritura descentrada que pretende crear una determinada ilusión de la realidad de un país en el que ya no se está, cuya lengua ya no se habla tal cual. Historia, lengua y país son recuerdos. Y el recuerdo . . . mueve el presente, lo desplaza, lo altera, lo saca de su centro".[9] Martini vivió y viajó en Europa. La idea del desplazamiento y el hombre como viajero aparece en *Composición de lugar* (1984), que transcurre en tres espacios: una ciudad española, otra italiana y una isla del delta argentino Paraná. El protagonista, Juan Minelli, descendiente de italianos, emprende desde Barcelona un viaje a Italia en busca de sus orígenes—es un viaje de vuelta seguido luego por un nuevo retorno a la Argentina en doble proceso de transculturación. Los otros autores hablan de fantasmas, Martini titula su novela *El fantasma imperfecto* (1985). El mismo protagonista de la anterior representa al viajero-héroe en crisis, el que se pregunta cuál es, y por qué, la historia que le ha tocado vivir.[10] El autor se aproxima a los mecanismos sociales con el esquema de la novela policial, pero la trasciende al incluir una problematización formal de la relación novelesca con la realidad. Lo que se busca es negar la verdad cotidiana para llegar a la pura verdad—la del sueño y la poesía; se logra a través del lenguaje que se convierte así en otro protagonista.

Martini no hace referencias específicas al país como los otros autores. El argumento lineal de la novela es sencillo: Minelli espera un avión en un aeropuerto—una "tierra de nadie"; recuerda y trata de entender un sueño, hace llamadas, vive un episodio erótico, es interrogado por la policía acerca de un crimen. Los personajes se observan, intercambian gestos mecánicos, a veces dicen unas palabras o cuentan una historia pero no se comunican. La imposibilidad de expresarse, la dificultad de comprender o el negarse a conocer la verdad convierten el lenguaje en la vía de manifestación del sentido total, en el mejor espejo de un deseo insaciable.[11] Martini transmite el clima opresivo, siniestro y despiadado de un mundo presidido por la violencia, la muerte y el absurdo. Cada autor a su modo, obviamente influido por el exilio, se convierte en "historiador"—como se clasifica a sí mismo Minelli—y además especializado en "historiografía" o sea un escritor especializado en el proceso de la escritura. Aclara Martini: "hay un más allá de la escritura que es lo que el escritor persigue. Algo siempre se le escapa. . . . la frustración provoca la energía indispensable para seguir intentando alcanzar ese algo—y así se escribe un libro".[12]

Comenta Michael Seidel en *Exile and the Narrative Imagination* (1986) que si un exiliado se define como alguien que habita un lugar y recuerda o proyecta la realidad de otro entonces el exilio para el escritor no es sólo un tema literario sino un constructor imaginativo fundamental.[13] El lugar en el tiempo se hace suelo exílico, habitable sólo a través de las aproximaciones de la memoria narrativa. La imaginación narrativa habita un dominio donde la ausencia es presencia. La experiencia exílica sirve de metáfora para la ficción en general donde se crean campos espaciales, temporales y textuales, es una metáfora para el estado de la imaginación narrativa en que el territorio deseado, perdido o encontrado es el destino narrativo—Martini lo ejemplifica.

Augusto Roa Bastos, refiriéndose a los escritores paraguayos sometidos al exilio, dice que están "anormalmente conscientes de los problemas de su sociedad pero también de su trabajo artístico" porque éste significa la necesidad de encarnar un destino, lo pueden hacer sólo "en el plano estético . . . de la palabra y de la escritura".[14] Según él, el arte de narrar no es sólo describir la realidad en palabras sino el arte de hacer que la palabra sea real; así "pueden superar su dramática situación de incomunicación y aislamiento para incorporarse en plenitud al conjunto de la literatura de habla hispana". Los argentinos también ejemplifican esto y así se incorporan con sus obras a esa "nación literaria del exilio" mencionada por Cortázar. Nos dan a entender que su literatura es mucho más que una crónica de represión y rebelión o autocrítica; es un vehículo para las corrientes literarias y la experimentación en la integración de concepto, técnica y estilo; presentan la realidad pero además la trascienden a través del acto de creación.

Notas

[1] Julio Cortázar, texto del discurso leído en la Universidad de Veracruz, titulado "De gladiadores y niños arrojados al río", reproducido en *Crisis*, abril 1986, pp. 40-42.

[2] Carlos A. Brocato, *El exilio es el nuestro* (Buenos Aires: Editorial Sudamericana, 1986), pp. 33, 79.

[3] Humberto Costantini, *En la noche* (Buenos Aires: Bruguera, 1985), pp. 30-31. Las citas en el texto provienen de esta edición y aparecen con págs. en paréntesis. Véase Elida Tendler, "Un hombre común y el cerco del terror", *Tiempo argentino*, diciembre 30, 1984, p. 7. Víctor Alvarez, "Costantini: entre el miedo y el exilio", *La Razón*, mayo 26, 1985, p. 12. Elvira Orphée, "La realidad y las normas del cuento", *La Nación*, julio 28, 1985, p. 4.

[4] Mempo Giardinelli, *El cielo con las manos* (Buenos Aires: Bruguera, 1985), p. 145. La 1ra. edición es de 1981. Las citas en el texto son de esta edición.

[5] Véase Mempo Giardinelli, "La democracia es un desafío a la creatividad" en *Magazine*, Año 1, N2, abril 19, 1985, pp. 90-91; también entrevista inédita con Reina Roffé, 1986.

[6] M. Vázquez Montalbán, "La nueva novela policíaca latinoamericana", *El país*, 30 de julio, 1984, p. 21.

[7] Véase Carlos Roberto Morán, "El cerco de la novela negra", *La Razón*, 1986, pp. 13-14.

[8] Mempo Giardinelli, *Qué solos se quedan los muertos* (Barcelona: Plaza y Janés Editores, 1986, 1ra. ed. 1985), p. 158. Las otras citas son de esta edición.

[9] En Pablo Cuezzo, "Los espacios de Juan Carlos Martini", *La Razón*, diciembre 29, 1985, pp. 6-7.

[10] Juan Carlos Martini, "¿Ha muerto el Boom? ¿Existe el Boom?", *Clarín*, noviembre 2, 1985, p. 3. También véase Pablo Cuezzo, *op. cit.*, p. 7.

[11] Véase Josefina Delgado, "El fugitivo fantasma de la novela", *La Razón*, junio 1, 1986; también Osvaldo Gallone, "Los textos del texto", *El periodista*,

Año 2, N92, 13-19 junio, 1986, p. 31. Asimismo Adolfo C. Martínez, *La Nación*, julio 14, 1985, p. 4. Roland Barthes es fuente de la idea sobre el lenguaje como espejo.

12 En artículo de Pablo Cuezzo, *op. cit.*, pp. 6-7.

13 Michael Seidel, *Exile and the Narrative Imagination* (New Haven: Yale University Press, 1986), pp. xii, 2, 4, 198, 199.

14 Augusto Roa Bastos, "La metáfora del exilio", *La Razón*, agosto 4, 1985, p. 11. Todas las citas en el texto son de esta página.

EXPATRIATION AND WRITING: JOSE DONOSO'S *EL JARDIN DE AL LADO*

Jonathan Tittler
Cornell University

Were I listening to this talk instead of giving it, I would most likely be asking myself whether the speaker was, either by experience or extensive research, qualified to expatiate on the theme announced in the title. Let me therefore hasten to announce to you, my true audience, that I have not suffered the pangs of either expulsion or incarceration, flight or ensconcement, in the normal sense of those terms, or even the "liminalization" that Gustavo Pérez Firmat evokes in his excellent recent book, *Literature and Liminality: Festive Readings in the Hispanic Tradition* (Durham: Duke University Press, 1986). Of course, Ithaca is not the jumping and funky New York City of my birth. Nor is New York, for that matter, in the least proximate to Jerusalem, so holy and hotly contested, where I presume my deeper roots to lie. But the fate of so many refugees in recent history—to become "restos tirados a la playa después de tan variados naufragios," as Donoso puts it—the fate of a Martí or a Lezama Lima, for better or worse, has not been mine.

Rather than a barrier to my capacity to understand the issues under scrutiny in this conference, however, I would like to argue that my lack of practical experience in this regard may turn out to be something of an asset. Most notably it permits me a dispassionate inspection of displacement and expatriation, particularly as they appear in José Donoso's recent novel, *El jardín de al lado* (1981), and especially as they relate to the question of writing, which is a space where I *have* dwelled with no little intensity for some time now. Please note that I do not speak of *emigration and exile* but *displacement and expatriation*, less familiar words that defuse somewhat the inherent emotional charge and divorce the memories and other associations from the terms under which we meet. I adopt this "clinical" approach not out of smug indifference but because Donoso's text presents itself as a case study of voluntary expatriation, a case we can measure against the situations of other contemporary Spanish-American writers. *El jardín de al lado*, which takes as its object and therefore distances itself from some of the works of the so-called Latin American "Boom," proves to be quite representative of the problematics of the authors who brought the Boom about.

Not precisely a novel of exile, nor even a novel of expatriation, *El jardín de al lado* is most essentially, at a certain level for the first-time reader, a novel of failure. It is within the sphere of failure that expatriation plays an important but no more than a supporting role. The symptoms of frustration and failure are ubiquitous. Julio Méndez, chronicler and protagonist of the tale, is a paunchy Chilean expatriate in his fifties who can barely support his family, with whom he moved to Spain after the fall of Allende. Suffering from severe self-doubt and insomnia, he seeks refuge in cognac and valium. His son Pato has left home because he cannot abide Julio's despotic tirades. With his wife Gloria he shares most notably a growing sexual indifference. But of greatest moment, Julio, a talented professor of English literature and a competent translator, is a failed writer. He cannot confront his typewriter, which inevitably throws his mediocrity back in his face. When he finally does, he falls prey to the temptation of a falsely exalted rhetoric of social protest (given his tepid political convictions) against Pinochet's military government, which once subjected him to a frightening six days of imprisonment. His sojourn in Spain, which was supposed to catalyze his liberation from the parochial precepts of the Chilean cultural milieu, instead leads him to a humiliating jailhouse of ineptitude. The novel's epilogue, a quotation from Cavafis, says it all: "No hallarás otra tierra ni otro mar./ La ciudad irá en ti siempre[. . .]/ La vida que aquí perdiste/ la has destruido en toda la tierra." More prosaically but perhaps more poignantly, Julio himself reflects, "Es curioso considerar cómo cada ser humano reproduce inevitablemente sus circunstancias, sea cual sea la localidad que transitoriamente habita. Arrastra consigo sus limitaciones" (p. 179).

Within the context of Julio's congenital insufficiency, the impact of mere geographic displacement is naturally, in his case, of only relative significance. To be sure, there are differences of degree, differences which the novel takes pains to respect. Julio suffers the pangs of nostalgia every time he encounters his wandering compatriots, every time he tastes a Chilean dish that is not quite the same as at home, every time he speaks with unbelievable clarity via satellite to his brother in Santiago. Those typical yearnings for an expatriate are complicated and made more acute by a sense of guilt with respect to his mother, who lies agonizing, waiting only for Julio's return before yielding to death's peaceful call. What cuts most deeply, however, is the linguistic estrangement he feels whenever he hears "coche" instead of "auto" and "piso" instead of "departamento"; or when he hears himself mouthing the phrase "mala cueva," that most grotesque of Chileanisms. Not dwelling in a context of Chilean Spanish, Julio rationalizes, impedes his novel's progress. The overwhelming sense of the *unheimlich* in their environment eventually pushes both Julio and Gloria to emotional crises in which their fragile personal identities threaten to fly apart. That they neither perish nor go mad may be attributed to nothing so much as the garden next door.

The garden of the novel's title is a *locus amoenus* which the troubled couple's apartment overlooks. Through a picture window Julio can project himself into that Edenic space, which reminds him of the garden of his youth, back in his mother's house in Santiago. This bridge of memory—a Bakhtinian *chronotope* which may well be the site of fiction—also functions as a passage to Julio's emotions, a trigger to his unconscious and, ultimately, an umbilical cord to his very origin. When Julio's mother dies and his brother threatens to sell the family house, garden and all, and with it to destroy Julio's precarious sense of self, it is the *jardín de al lado*, the proxy paradise, that provides the mucilage for his centrifugal psyche. At the same time, however, it is Julio's marginal position with regard to that secure enclosure (he never so much as sets foot in it) that serves as an index for his incapacity to return to his origins, to reduce his self-deluding internal distance, and to participate guiltlessly in Chilean history. In mankind's fallen state, the novel would appear to assert, not even art can get us back to Ithaca.

Instead, and I quote from a talk Donoso gave, in English, on the prospect of returning to one's point of departure, "The homeland of a writer is not really a place, but a language. Not even a language, but a certain section, a fraction of that language which one identifies with. The return voyage to Ithaca is an effort to regain one's vernacular, which the intervening silence of years and space has rendered powerless, and plug into it again, even when one lives abroad" ("Ithaca: The Impossible Return," *The City College Papers*, Number 18, February 1980, p. 11). Finding one's voice, one's lost language with which to posit credibly a sense of one's absence, is thus the contemporary answer to Odysseus' perennial plight. In fact, Donoso states elsewhere in that same lecture, "I think it is this lack of the immediacy of the pressing public reality, this perspective, the time and the void for the imagination to grow in and to preen and prattle and prance, to be free and subjective, that has given the novel of my generation, written in un-useful and un-heroic style, its character and its stature" (p. 10). Julio's failure, then, stems from his inability to consider his inevitable disenfranchisement as perhaps the source of his greatest strength. By confusing literature with self-serving political action and by writing in a full-blown, Romanticized prose that deceives only himself, he virtually assures his condemnation to literary oblivion.

Enter Gloria. No less displaced than Julio, and, as a woman, certainly more disenfranchised than he, since her upper-class formation prepared her to be nothing more than an appendage to her husband, Gloria nonetheless sees things with a different pair of eyes. She understands the potential advantages of being in the here and now, at a distance from the womb: the possibility of growing, of discovering new values and perspectives, and, most important, of adopting new masks. Instead of vainly seeking a naive authenticity, Gloria espouses the deployment of an emancipating imposture. This quality, not quite parenthetically, is perhaps the single most pervasive aspect of Donoso's fiction, as Ricardo Gutiérrez Mouat has shown in his impressive study *José Donoso: Impostùra e impostación* (Gaithersburg, MD: Hispamérica, 1984 [?]). What I am insinuating is that—and anyone familiar with the novel can corroborate my response—in one of the most refreshing peripities to be found in contemporary fiction, the "real" author of Julio's saga of failure turns out to be Gloria. That is, the novel is neither Julio's saga nor is it a tale of failure. Instead of a geographic displacement that leads to defeat, this up-to-date version of Golden Age Spain's *mujer en disfraz varonil* entails a sexual expatriation (a wrenching displacement if ever there was one) which, by portraying the failure of writing *in* writing, recuperates a sense of provisional wholeness without pretending to convey transcendent truth. "Al fin y al cabo," says a narratorial voice of uncertain gender, "uno no escribe con el propósito de decir algo, sino para saber qué quiere decir y para qué y para quiénes" (p. 159). Within the fiction it is travesty—with the full weight of its transgressive gaiety—that galvanizes Gloria's identity as a successful writer and as a person who feels "bien dans sa peau."

Gloria's wellbeing leads me back to my point of departure, the thesis that emigration does no more than maintain the appearance of causality where *angst* and failure are concerned, at least for the talented voluntary exile. As a sagacious parting performative gesture with respect to authorial distance, Donoso discloses the time and place of his writing as "Calaceite, verano 1980" (p. 264). Ironically, then, but with total consistency within the system of the text, this reflection on peripatetic Chileans who find themselves stranded in Madrid was written in Cataluña, where the author resided for many years before returning to

Chile later in this decade. Moreover, his cosmopolitan vision and willingness to engage in formal experimentation (aspects of his fiction even more in evidence in *El lugar sin límites* and *El obsceno pájaro de la noche* than in the novel under discussion) locate him squarely within the tendencies of the novelists generally acknowledged as constituing the leadership of the *nueva novela hispanoamericana*: Julio Cortázar, Carlos Fuentes, Gabriel García Márquez, and Mario Vargas Llosa. Despite the clear distinctions among these authors along the political axis (Cortázar and García Márquez occupying the left, Vargas Llosa the center, and Fuentes the left-center), all of them have used expatriation to exceedingly good avail. They have globalized and revitalized the Latin American narrative both thematically and technically, much as Neruda, Huidobro, and Vallejo did for poetry earlier in the century. Some, as in the cases of Donoso and Vargas Llosa, have returned to their homelands. Others, such as Fuentes and García Márquez, have continued to live abroad, where their productivity and influence have in no way diminished.

Cortázar, of course, died almost two years ago at his adoptive home in France, signalling the beginning of the end of an era. Some displace Latin American narrators of the next generation—Antonio Skármeta and the Cuban Reinaldo Arenas are two outstanding examples—show themselves to be considerably more exercised than their predecessors about their nomadic plight, and one would be wrong to dismiss their allegations lightly. But it should be clear that, if nothing else, what both these angry young men have been spared so far is the very special sort of exile reserved for *re*patriates, the estranging experience of returning home to find it is something less or other than what it was when they left. Or perhaps it is we who are less; whichever way one cares to take it, outside of stories of the "Hansel and Gretel" and "Jack and the Beanstalk" sort, Donoso tells and shows us artfully, that comfortable, warm, protected space called home is not ours to know, even if we never travel. Another younger novelist, the Colombian expatriate Rafael Humberto Moreno-Durán, has phrased all this as felicitously as one can: "El exilio para mí es una metáfora de otra metáfora. La metáfora del escritor, que es exiliado por naturaleza, que se casa con la soledad y se asila en la página en blanco" (*El Colombiano* [10/3/86] p. 5).

Before returning to my own garden adjacent to Ithaca—which in a very important sense is not the same one I left in order to come to this conference, nor am I the same person who undertook the journey—I would like to add one more reflection to what is turning into something of an apology for Donoso. The main point, I think, is that no apologies are necessary. The Chilean master makes manifest through his symbols that it is inevitable to yearn for home, childhood, truth, and security, all of which we are barred from knowing fully. But the marvelous side of this harsh reality is that the empty space torn open at the loss of these cherished values is the very place of creativity. Through the creative imagination—which rushes to fill that void—we can see as readers what we have not witnessed and understand what we have not by ourselves conceived. Despite its seeming paradoxicality, what binds contemporary men and women together, more than politics, more than ideology, is their deep seated alienation, their sense of unwholeness and marginality. It is this discomfiting peripheral status that equalizes inveterate travelers with stay-at-homes, Anglos with Latinos. José Donoso evidently feels that lack of plenitude sharply and, as an author, works feverishly to compensate for it, writing in *El jardín de al lado* both within and about such a metaphysical absence. To what higher social calling may a writer aspire?

MEMORIES OF HOMELAND IN CARPENTIER'S *EL REINO DE ESTE MUNDO*

Margaret V. Ekstrom
St. John Fisher College

The journey of the Cuban author Alejo Carpentier to Haiti in 1943 and its subsequent effects on his literary production are quite well-documented.[1] *El reino de este mundo*, published in 1949, is a fictionalized account of the Haitian Revolution (1789-1804) and its aftermath. Although rooted in historical fact, the work is actually a stylized evocation of the past.[2] The theme of memory is a dominant one: memories of a lost or distant homeland, yearnings for ethnic origins, a search for identity and cultural awareness—all are seen in all of the major characters in the work. It has been called an origin-obsessed history[3] as the characters attempt to recover those lost cultural roots.

Carpentier himself was well aware of the importance of ethnic heritage, since he was born in Cuba of French and Russian ancestry and since he was often absent from his home island during times of study and travel. In the very famous "Prólogo" to *El reino de este mundo*,[4] Carpentier describes how deeply he was affected by what he had learned of Haitian history and culture, and he emphasizes the significance of Caribbean music and ceremonies in the cultural development of the region. All of these elements enter into the work under discussion here.

At the very beginning of *El reino de este mundo,* in Chapter I of Part I, some of the main characters approach the theme of memory. The young black slave, Ti Noel, whose reminiscences link the major developments of the work, has just begun to awaken to his cultural heritage. Apparently born and raised in Haiti, he has based his images of Africa on the descriptions he has heard from his friend, the powerful Mandinga slave Mackandal.[5] The exotic names of African kingdoms (Arada, Angola) and gods (Dá, Adonhueso, Muza) have stirred the imagination of the young Haitian. The pale and weak European kings seem to him to be no match for the mighty African rulers who were at once warriors, hunters and priests. Those were leaders from the "Gran Allá," the distant African homeland, men who could converse with the forces of nature and who would one day rise up in defense of their followers in the Caribbean.

The theme continues in Chapter II, when Mackandal paints more of his magical pictures of Africa, the cities of Guinea in particular—myths, legends, ceremonies, music—all seem to come to life. This figure is the same historical Mackandal who used his skill with poisons to plan one of the principal rebellions against the French rule in Haiti.[6] After his friend has escaped and run away to develop his revolt, Ti Noel deeply misses Mackandal's stories and the world they had evoked. The youth is delighted when he is invited to participate in the secret plot, as Mackandal is revealed as a high priest, the Lord of Venom, determined to put an end to white rule and to establish a great empire of free blacks.[7] Part of Mackandal's powerful attraction lies in the energy of African story—telling, as he persuades others to follow him.[8] But the full extent of his powers becomes clear in subsequent chapters, with references to omens, gods, cyclical metamorphosis, magically evocative names (Damballah, Ogún) and the forces of nature.

After hiding for some four years following the poison episode, the mysterious Mackandal returns in a changed form in Chapter VII, during the preparations for Christmas. The cultural variations of the mix of French and African heritage are apparent as each group celebrates their savior. Mackandal is given a litany of heroic names as the expected one who will alleviate the sufferings of his people. Although Mackandal is eventually captured and executed by the French, his people believe that he was truly able to escape by changing his form and that he has kept his promise to remain in the kingdom of this world. There are indeed African liberation myths of Yoruba-bred heroes who escape by flying away.[9]

The theme of memory and origins surfaces once again in Part II, with the first chapter providing additonal information on Ti Noel's master, Monsieur Lenormand de Mezy. Having outlived two wives, the land-owner has taken up with a French actress, Mademoiselle Floridor, who persuades him to pay a visit to Paris. After a few months, something unexpected happens; he finds himself nostalgic for Haiti, missing the sun and open spaces of his island domain; his return to France has not been the key to happiness which he had envisioned.[10] And so the couple returns to Haiti.

Some twenty years have passed between parts one and two. Ti Noel has fathered a dozen children, to whom he has imparted the stories of

Africa and the legends of Mackandal. The cultural origins, the ethnic heritage, have thus been preserved. Monsieur Lenormand de Mezy has fallen into a sort of drunken mania. The neglected and ailing Mademoiselle Floridor lives in her crazed memories of imagined dramatic triumphs.

The decadent French culture in Haiti is contrasted with the vibrant African one, yearning to be free. The Jamaican Bouckman has come to Haiti with news of the French Revolution, encouraging the slaves to rise up in the name of their African gods and claim their rightful freedom. Again the evocative names of the ancestral deities are chanted: Damballah, Ogún, Changó, Kankanikán, Batala, Panamá, Bakulé, Radá, Badagrí.[11]

Monsieur Lenormand de Mezy is of course opposed to the French Revolution which has brought notions of liberty, fraternity and equality to the slaves of Haiti. He believes that the Peninsular French know nothing about conditions on the island and should not meddle in Haitian affairs. But the slaves have already risen up in rebellion, destroying lands and property, killing some of the landowners. Bouckman is eventually executed, the revolt crushed and some of the rebellious slaves punished. The French leaders on the island have devised a plan to exterminate all the blacks, but they have not considered the power of African religion (Vaudoux or Vodun) in opposition. The cultivated French had no intention of concerning themselves with a secret African cult.[12] Rather than risk the loss of his slaves, which represent all his wealth after the destruction of his plantation, Monsieur Lenormand de Mezy decides to leave Haiti and seek refuge in Santiago de Cuba.

The Chapter V description of the French emigré colony in Cuba is yet another example of the theme of memory. It is of course a time of emigration and exile for the French who have fled from the rebellions in Haiti. They set up their own little world, a microcosm of French Haiti transplanted to Santiago, with their theater, their food, their parties, their music, their dress style—all of which influenced the Cuban culture in due course. Monsieur Lenormand de Mezy is shown spending most of his time gambling away what was left of his fortune. But for Ti Noel, also in a state of enforced exile, the experience proves much more rewarding. He is impressed by the Spanish lifestyle and by the Hispanic version of religion as represented by the Cathedral of Santiago: in the warrior patron saint of the Spanish he finds a warm kinship with his mighty African gods.[13]

The last two chapters of Part II contain an interlude referring to the visit of Paulina Bonaparte, the sister of Napoleon, and her husband,

General Leclerc, to Haiti; they have been sent to the island by the French government to investigate the rebellion and to gain orderly political control. The episode is interesting in terms of the romantic image of tropical life which Paulina has conjured up out of literary references. Once in Haiti, she falls under the influence of Solimán, an African servant, who tries to protect her from an epidemic of tropical fever by teaching her magical African rituals. Eventually, Leclerc dies and Paulina leaves for Rome, taking with her an amulet to the god Papá Legba, crafted by Solimán. Haiti sinks into a deeper condition of chaos, but the boats filled with dogs and venomous snakes sent to the island by the French landowners exiled in Cuba are unsuccessful. The moment seems propitious for the triumph of the African deities.

Part III opens some time later, in the early years of the 1800's, during the rule of Henri Christophe in Haiti. An old but sturdy Ti Noel has gradually earned his freedom in Cuba, after serving under a criollo master who was preferible to his French one. He has saved enough money to book passage for a return to Haiti, the homeland he wishes to see now that it has abolished slavery. He has enhanced his magical powers over the years, developing the talent to converse with animals, inanimate objects or the forces of nature. Although the omens upon his arrival are full of warnings, he falls to his knees and gives thanks for the joy of returning to his homeland, where the legendary African gods have at last proven themselves triumphant (or so he believes).[14] He returns past the caves of Mackandal to the hacienda of Monsieur Lenormand de Mezy—and he finds the place in ruins. He is conscripted by black soldiers dressed in Napoleonic style to carry bricks for the construction of a great fortress being built under orders of King Henri Christophe. Ti Noel is shocked to discover that blacks are still doing forced labor in Haiti, but now the overseers and masters are other blacks. This situation seems incredible to him, for apparently the revolution only succeeded in substituting one set of masters for another. The cultural glory and triumph he has so long anticipated has still not materialized.

The irony of the situation is compounded by the construction of the fortress itself, which is being built in European colonial style by Haitian blacks who work as virtual slaves for their black king who was once a chef. The blood of sacrificial bulls is mixed with mortar for the construction so that the fortress will be invulnerable, in a series of rituals performed in the presence of the statues of classical warriors, a Spanish cannon, French plaques and Latin inscriptions. The cultural clash is as much in evidence as ever.

Finally able to escape from the construction work, Ti Noel is drawn back once again to the old hacienda, where he lives a precarious existence among the ruins. He manages a return visit to the cape city he had seen several times in his youth, on journeys with his master, but he finds it in a state of decadence, full of rumors of the cruelties of the king, full of omens of impending death. Ti Noel returns home singing a song of insults to a king, any king. The importance of music in cultural awareness is again in evidence.[15] The next three chapters show its effects on the king.

During mass, Henri Christophe is haunted by the ghost of his former confessor, Cornejo Breille, who was condemned to death because he knew too much about the king. The ailing ruler is assisted by his servant Solimán, but he still hears the processions of musicians in the streets, playing African rhythms. The king realizes his error in trying to be too European, in being false to his African origins. As fires rage near the palace, as the drums beat in the distance, the king commits suicide (historically in 1820). His body is encased in mortar within the great fortress as another episode concludes in Haitian history.

However, in the shorter Part IV, Carpentier resolves some of the crises for his characters. The remnants of the Haitian royal family have taken refuge in Rome, accompanied by Solimán, who has become much admired in the city for his highly embellished tales of Haitian history. Somewhat drunk one night, he comes upon the statue of a beautiful woman, which he mistakes for the body of his beloved former mistress Paulina Bonaparte. Crazed with fever, Solimán ignores the attentions of an Italian physician and prays in Haitian French to his distant, ancient African gods—he is a man haunted by his memories and his cultural conflicts.

Meanwhile, back in Haiti, Ti Noel has established his own little mad yet benevolent realm on the ruins of the hacienda. Surrounded by the relics of the past glories of Henri Christophe, taken from the ransacked palace, and of Monsieur Lenormand de Mezy, Ti Noel talks constantly to everyone and everything. He believes that he has an as yet unknown mission to fulfill, and he is awaiting a sign for what it is. He is respected by his neighbors for his years, his experience, his magical powers, his general benevolence and his parties, where everyone receives an honorary title in one of the orders of nature.[16] He is horrified when his domain is measured by official surveyors, who represent the new republican government. He realizes that he is now witnessing what Mackandal and Bouckman had not foreseen—the rule of mulattoes over blacks. Desperate, Ti Noel begins to have powerful memories of Mackandal; he realizes that he too has the power to transform himself into another shape. His metamorphoses include bird, burro, wasp, ant, goose. He discovers that all these creatures have characteristics in common with man. But he decides that he should remain in human form, to accept the challenges of life on earth, to defy the latest group of new would-be masters and to work toward a better life. During a sudden hurricane, Ti Noel is swept away by a great green wind, never to be known of again, at least in that form.

Thus it can be seen that Carpentier has skillfully interwoven in his work the themes of history and memory, exile and return, ethnic origins and cultural identity. Some critics have commented that the compression and speed of the narrative is a reflection of the quick pace of history in the Caribbean.[17] It could however be said that, given recent events in Haiti, the island's history has progressed very slowly in terms of changes beneficial to the majority of the people. The search for a national identity is a frequent theme throughout Latin American literature—and Haiti has proven to be no exception, with its French, African and Hispanic heritage. Ti Noel can be viewed as a representative of an awakening black cultural awareness in the Caribbean.[18] His ultimate wisdom comes through the ancestral truths which he had learned from Mackandal; his mysterious powers reflect a deep cultural comprehension of the natural forces which surround him.[19] He exemplifies a phenomenon found in Haiti of a collective faith in a wider dimension of reality than Western rationalism accepts.[20] Within African tradition, individuals seek self-realization and social validation by fulfilling duties and exercising rights within that tradition.[21] Within Afro-Antillean folklore, there is a search for the fusion of self and history, "a quest for origins in the natural fusion of history and consciousness in a utopian past."[22] Although he tried to recover his ethnic past through an exercise of cultural memory, Ti Noel eventually replaced the myth of a utopian past with the perhaps equally intangible myth of a better future, at the conclusion of *El reino de este mundo*. We may say of him that "a foreign or absent Mother culture has always cradled his judgement."[23] And assuredly the theme of return to origins has found a superior spokesman in the person of Ti Noel's literary creator, Alejo Carpentier, who brought a deep and informed cultural awareness to his writings.

Notes

[1] Donald Leslie Shaw, *Alejo Carpentier* (Boston: Twayne Publishers, 1985), Introduction and pp. 26-34. For discussions of the mythification of history, see: John S. Brushwood, *The Spanish-American Novel: A Twentieth Century*

Survey (Austin and London: University of Texas Press, 1975), pp. 170-173 and Seymour Menton, *Prose Fiction of the Cuban Revolution* (Austin and London: University of Texas Press, 1975), pp. 48 and 191.

[2] Raimundo Lazo, *La literatura cubana* (México: UNAM Manuales universitarios, 1965), pp. 204-205 and Edmundo Desnoes, editor, *Los dispositivos en la flor. Cuba: literatura desde la revolución* (Hanover, N.H.: Ediciones del Norte, 1981), p. 3.

[3] Roberto González Echevarría, *Alejo Carpentier: The Pilgrim at Home* (Ithaca and London: Cornell University Press, 1977), pp. 26 and 107.

[4] Alejo Carpentier, *El reino de este mundo* (México: Compañía general de ediciones, 1969), pp. 7-17.

[5] *Ibid.*, p. 27.

[6] Thomas Ott, *The Haitian Revolution 1789-1804* (Knoxville: University of Tennessee Press, 1973), p. 18.

[7] Carpentier, *op cit.*, p. 50.

[8] *Ibid.*, pp. 61, 65-66 and José Piedra, "A Return to Africa with a Carpentier Tale" in MLN - *Modern Language Notes* (March, 1982), 97: 2, p. 404.

[9] Piedra, *Ibid.*

[10] Carpentier, *Ibid.*, p. 73.

[11] *Ibid.*, pp. 78-79.

[12] *Ibid.*, pp. 90-91 and James G. Leyburn, *The Haitian People* (New Haven and London: Yale University Press, 1966), Part II on religion, pp. 131-160.

[13] Carpentier, *Ibid.*, pp.98-99.

[14] Roberto González Echevarría, "Literature of the Hispanic Caribbean" in *Latin American Literary Review*: Special Issue on Hispanic Caribbean Literature, Carnegie-Mellon University of Pittsburgh, Pennsylvania (Spring-Summer, 1980), Vol. VIII, Number 16, pp. 2-3 and Carpentier, *op. cit.*, p. 121.

[15] González Echevarría, "Literature of the Hispanic Caribbean," pp. 12-13, 17.

[16] Carpentier, *op. cit.*, p. 184.

[17] Shaw, *op. cit.*, p. 33 and González Echevarría, "Literature . . . ," pp. 2-3.

[18] For works on this theme, see Miriam De Costa, editor, *Blacks in Hispanic Literature* (Port Washington, N.Y.: Kennikat Press, 1977), p. 81 and William Luis, editor, *Voices from Under: Black Narrative in Latin America and the Caribbean* (Westport, Conn.: Greenwood Press, 1984).

[19] Pedro M. Barreda-Tomás, "Alejo Carpentier: Dos visiones del negro, dos conceptos de la América" in *Hispania* (1972), 55: 34-44, p. 41. For a fuller treatment, see also by the same author: *The Black Protagonist in the Cuban Novel*, translated by Page Bancroft (Amherst: University of Massachusetts Press, 1979).

[20] Shaw, *op. cit.*, pp. 27 and 101.

[21] Piedra, *op. cit.*, p. 402.

[22] González Echevarría, *Alejo Carpentier: Pilgrim*, pp. 186, 212, 230.

[23] George Lamming, *The Pleasures of Exile,* cited by González Echevarría in "Literature of the Hispanic Caribbean," *op. cit.*, p. 4.

THE EXPERIENCE OF EXILE IN JAVIER CAMPOS' POETRY

Irene B. Hodgson
Xavier University

Testimony as a literary genre and the perspective of the exile have profoundly affected Latin American literature since the mid 1970's. This decade, however, is not the first in Latin America to provide testimony in its cultural manifestations of repression or of life in foreign lands and spaces, but it is, certainly, a period in which the expulsion of people from their own countries has become massive in scale. The brief ascension to power of popular governments in the southern cone (Chile, Uruguay) during that decade was suppressed by uprisings of their militaries supported by those with political and financial interests (i.e., the U.S. government, the C.I.A., multinational firms). Afterwards, there was an intensification of repression, tortures, the radical elimination of the labor unions, of cultural organizations and of institutions, the expulsion of thousands of people, including workers, middle class, professionals and intellectuals.

Testimonial literature has become a *leit-motiv* for many of the writers who became aware of and lived these situations. Through these writings, they tell the reader of the tortures, detentions and interrogations of the military repression (for example: Hernán Valdés, *Tejas verdes: diario de un campo de concentración*).[1]

Exile, on the other hand, implies time, time lived in another country that is not the native one. It is the new place where one arrives, almost by chance, without much prior choice and not at all like in a trip designed by a travel agency.

Testimonial literature and literature of exile, according to Julio Cortázar, seems to be of two recurrent types: an almost sick nostalgia for the country that one no longer lives in or that no longer exists and the idyllic reconstruction in some nebulous future of what has been lost.[2]

Javier Campos is one of the poets that Soledad Bianchi in her anthology *Entre la lluvia y el arco iris: Algunos poetas jóvenes chilenos* (Rotterdam, 1983) includes in what she calls a "generación dispersa" o "diezmada," a scattered, destroyed generation, comparable to the Generation of 1936 in Spain, produced in Chile as a result of the military coup in 1973, "scattered" because of the distance and the gulf between those who stayed in Chile and those who went to other parts of the world.[3]

Javier Campos has published poetry, short stories and critical articles in Chile, the United States and Spain. He was unable to continue teaching at the University of Concepción perhaps partly because of an article called "Poesía y proceso revolucionario" published only a week before the coup. His first book of poetry, *Las moscas y Las banderas*, was to have been published by a literary magazine on September 11, 1973, the very day of the coup. His two published books of poetry are *Las últimas fotografías* (Montevideo, 1981) and *La ciudad en llamas* published July 1986 in Chile in a bilingual Spanish/English edition with an introduction by Soledad Bianchi.[4] *Las últimas fotografías* occurs in the repressive atmosphere of the first years of the military dictatorship. *La ciudad en llamas* represents what we could call a third perspective (neither the nostalgia nor reconstruction Cortázar mentions) of life during the "second exile," that is, once the basic needs for food and shelter, etc. have been met and some acceptation or assimilation has begun.

The two books *Las últimas fotografías* and *La ciudad en llamas* reflect two very different moments in Campos' experience of exile. Most of the first book was written in Chile between 1976 and 1977. Although Campos remained in Chile during the years immediately following the military coup, his isolation resulting from his position against the military government produced an interior exile.

When he left Chile, the poems he brought with him to the United States were photographs of Chile. They are yellowed and musty. They show a decayed past and an equally devastated future. Wedding photos show the bride with musty flowers. In a corner, she runs toward a man with dark glasses in a wheel chair. Not only has her past decayed but her future is blind and crippled. Her past and future are those of her country, Chile. Campos' photographs, that is, his poems, record a past that has been destroyed by the military government and a future that is bleak.

The most immediate subject of Chilean poetry, written both in and outside Chile, after the 1973 military coup had to be the situation of Chile and of the Chilean people. The junta's takeover affected every aspect of life, not merely the political and the economic. The poetry reflects this, as the poets express the realities which surround them, perhaps without understanding the full implications of what they see.

Under a repressive government such as that of the Chilean junta, writers and artists, still in the country but spiritually exiled from it, turn to new forms of expression in order to circumvent the censorship. Writers tend to use more difficult language, more metaphors and symbols to disguise and thereby protect their true meaning. As the writer becomes more isolated (in his interior exile), his poetry becomes elitist in the sense that it belongs to a group of kindred spirits who understand and identify with the message the poet is trying to convey. Those writers who end up outside of Chile, because they have to, or choose to, leave, can express themselves more clearly without the same fear of reprisals.

Different poets have chosen different ways to express the realities around them. Javier Campos has used a photographic image to convey the destruction of the cities and the persecution of the people in them. He chose to use photographic imagery in his writings precisely at a time when many Chileans were burning photographs and other objects which might compromise or incriminate them—and shortly after a journalist filmed his own death as he was shot by soldiers.

In his book *Las últimas fotografías*, published in Uruguay in 1981, Javier Campos records scenes as if viewed through the eye of a daguerrotype camera. The camera image, as Campos uses it in *Las últimas fotografías*, suggests multiple levels of interpretation. On the most superficial level, the camera is a recording device, taking photographs of withered dreams and bullet-scarred buildings, providing a record (a photo essay) of the present destruction which will perhaps be concealed later. But the camera also functions as a weapon in Campos' hands. In photographing the situation, recording it on film and on paper, he takes a position. The photographs, that is, the poems, are his statement of protest.

On yet another level, the camera is also identified with another type of arm, the hand-held machine gun used by the soldiers. When Campos describes "la máquina" in the final poem of the book, he mixes images of camera and machine guns and thus describes both. The machine is small and black; its aperture measures 1.2 or more. It measures space and in order to reach a faraway object, one uses a telephoto lens or a telescopic sight. A man can reach a head, or a hand or a heart—by surprise. There is an almost imperceptible click when he depresses the shutter or trigger. Something opens and closes, taking in the image sighted. This machine can be hung from a shoulder or a belt or carried in a case, and then it has to be reloaded in a secret place when it can fire no more shots.

Since almost all the images in the poem suggest a machine gun while seeming to describe a camera, this camera becomes sinister, an instrument of death. The negatives are locked up like the prisoners; later, they are thrown away when they are no longer useful. Once these records are turned over to his superiors, the photographer (or soldier) is promoted and then goes back out into the streets.

This three-way use of the camera is clearly seen in a short poem, "Hacia los edificios":

> Hacia los edificios
> Como si buscara objetos perdidos
> y cuando revelan el negativo
> Los edificios están agujereados de balas
> También se oyen gritos y sirenas. (p. 19)

The machine is the camera which takes the photograph of the buildings. It is the gun that the soldiers point at the buildings and fire at them, thus riddling them with bullet holes. It is, in addition, the tool or weapon the poet uses to reveal what has happened to the city.

In the introductory poem, the image is not static and therefore suggests a movie camera. Beggars fill the streets but they are not well received by the people of the city. As time passes, the 1000 days of the Allende government, hopes fade; the people age and tire of being reminded by the beggars of their forgotten dreams. People celebrated in the streets when Allende won the 1970 election; Campos mixes those celebrants with the uncertain people who fill the streets in the days before the coup and with those who vote to support Allende in March of 1973, only months before their dreams are shattered in September by the coup (pp. 5-7).

The poems which follow correspond to two different moments in Campos' poetry. The first poems were written in Chile and the imagery is more obscure. The tranquility is only apparent; the reality portrayed is sad. The photographs themselves are shadowy, shot in the semi-darkness, printed in faded colors and sepia tones. There is an air of old age: the flowers are withered, the atmosphere mouldy and decayed, the darkness increasing. The men and women in these poems are old: their dreams have faded and their hopes vanished. They are blind and crippled, with dark glasses, white canes and wheel chairs (pp. 9-15).

In other poems, Campos describes a search for a beloved who has disappeared. But this is not just love poetry,but rather an extension of Roberto Fernández Retamar's identification of love and revolution imagery, for, on another level, the loved one represents the thousands or any *one*, of the "desaparecidos," those who were (and are) imprisoned or killed without anyone knowing what has happened to them.

The later poems in the book were written after Campos came to the United States in 1977. They are longer and less obscure, reflecting the tendency of a writer who is exiled or takes refuge in another country to change the style of his writing once he no longer must cloak in obscurity what he wishes to express. Even so, Campos never makes a direct political reference.

He continues to use suggestion, implied comparison, ambiguity and multiple levels of meaning to convey his message to the reader. Many images in this poetry refer to interrogation, torture and persecution. In the poem: "He perdido la voz . . . ", some of the verbs are commands: "Enciendan las luces/ Hagan una hoguera." The lights being turned on suggest a nocturnal police raid; the bonfires are to burn books. Later in the poem, there is a suggestion of an interrogation being held and of the subject having to be hospitalized or of a patrol vehicle with its flashing lights roaming the streets, ever vigilant: "Qué es eso que se PRENDE y APAGA/ Por qué hay tantas sirenas de ambulancias" (p. 21). Another poem tells of a race of homosexual horses held on September 18, 1974, Chilean independence day a full year after the coup. Images are reminiscent of the testimonies which describe prisoners being told to lie on their faces and spread their legs while they are kicked and beaten or hung up while their legs are broken. This poem may also refer to accounts of forced masturbation and homosexual acts or of women violated before the eyes of their husbands or brothers.

As in Gonzalo Millán's long poem, "La ciudad," images of developing and printing photographs suggest the electric shocks described in the testimonies, and more specifically, the wet paper reminds us of people drenched with water before the current is applied to their bodies.

In yet another poem, Campos says "la muerte manipula las películas."

Campos' poems which use the photographic image as a literary device make the reader share his sorrow and anger about what has happened and continues to happen in his country.

In his most recent book, *La ciudad en llamas*, Campos responds to his experience in the United States. As already mentioned, according to Julio Cortázar, most poetry in exile concentrates on the past (an idealized past) or a future reconstruction of the country. Campos, however, writes about his experience in and encounter with the new country. The speaker is a man who was forced by circumstance to come to another country where he never wanted to be. His encounter with the

American city is portrayed through encounters with women ("Conocí a una mujer Bella en esta ciudad . . . ," "Me enamoré de una mujer que conocí en un bar . . . "). These women lead him and make love to him ("Me guió. . . . Me besó. . . . Me acarició. . . . "). The speaker is usually passive in these encounters; they happen *to* him. His only decisive action seems to be when he leaves, for he cannot, will not, commit himself to any of these relationships. He will eventually leave ("yo no me detendré en esas ciudades ardiendo"). The poems say that the door (to these relationships) opens gently but closes violently.

Images often continue to be yellowed, musty or dark as in the earlier book. The light in these poems is the fire produced by the city lights at night, the lighted signs, the advertising which glorifies life in the consumer society. The signs show what one "needs" to be happy. It creates a world of unreality, of illusion, reflected in the repeated film and dream imagery, for films, like advertisements, create an imaginary world (a dream world). The films in these poems are silent films and some of the images evoke specific films, such as the eye in Picasso and Dali's "The Andalusian Dog," lighted signs in Jean-Jacques Beineix's "Moon in the Gutter" and the concept of previous generations housed in a swimming pool in Ron Howard's "Cocoon." The protagonist and the women are seen as actors, or as "estrellas" (stars), images which link them to the lights and the illusions they produce.

The woman also sometimes is identified as death as in the previous book ("Sentada en su automóvil en llamas/ Se quedó fuera/ Tan bella/ La muerte"). In this book, that imagery suggests that yielding to the woman, the city, is a kind of death. Yet each rejection of the woman increases the protagonist's isolation and loneliness. His suitcase, which represents his exiled condition (Skarmeta indicates that keeping a suitcase packed, ready to leave, is characteristic of the exile), grows long as a train. Images of trains and passengers reinforce the idea of the transience of the exile's presence. The trains are comparable to those in Arreola's story "El guardagujas." Passengers may wait for years; the park becomes a station filled with unused tickets. Men and women may never sit across from one another (that is, make contact) in the train. They see each other only through plastic doors. Space travel imagery also identifies astronauts as isolated beings, travelers in empty space.

Other images Campos uses are of desires and dreams, both of which come out at night to roam the city with the exile. Campos has said that the dreams in *La ciudad en llamas* are not a photographic experience of conscious reality—dreams are collages of experiences, places, people from different moments—past, present or a possible future. They are "situaciones o escenas múltiples y compactas que pueden señalar *deseos latentes* (Freud) del presente del pasado o del futuro."[5] Thus they merge the idealized and not so ideal past and an imaged future (though perhaps not the ideal one Cortázar speaks of) with a not always pleasant present. The speaker's dreams are musty or crushed. Yet even if the desires or dreams are vivid, they are clearly unreal, illusory; they can never come true.

Aristóbulo Pardo has suggested a certain surrealism in the long poem of *Las últimas fotografías*; Soledad Bianchi compares some of Campos' images (such as that of the suitcase that becomes a train) to Magritte and another of a girl flying through a window like a great sleepy bee to Chagall (p. 17).

The new country and its cities are also portrayed as prisons. Images which were connected with to the police and torture in *Las últimas fotografías* are repeated here: flashing lights ("luces que se prenden y apagan") this time relate to advertisements but also suggest the other connotation to one who has read Campos' earlier work. In a poem about Nevada, he talks about machines that make people disappear (the illusions created in Reno can destroy the possibilities of real life). In one poem, the speaker says directly: "Tú eres una prisión gigante. . . . "). He is trapped in a world of which he never asked to be a part. He emphasizes two specific negative realities of this country: he speaks of how the undocumented workers work "de rodillas" (that is, on their knees), an image of the discrimination and elitism of the United States; the white train which carries "las armas de la muerte" (i.e., the arms of death) is the famous white train crossing this country with nuclear weapons as its cargo, an instrument of war, death and destruction.

However, the exile's reactions to the new city are not all negative. The ambivalence of his feelings are indicated in contradictory imagery, such as "nieve ardiente" and "nieve candente." The snow which is traditionally cold is usually burning in these poems. The speaker mixes images of paradise, purgatory and hell.

The speaker knows that he cannot go back in time. His native land (when he is able to again live in it) will not be the same and he cannot communicate with his past (or people from it) satisfactorily now. The mailmen are ancient, the letters are eventually returned or are undeliverable because the address is unknown. They travel on a white train, their arrival and consequent communication, therefore, hopeless.

The book, *La ciudad en llamas*, is a discouraging expression of the experience of exile. While the exile is aware that he cannot be in his country and is grateful to be able to be somewhere else (in Campos's short story, "Agua final," like Campos, to be a professor in an American university), he still yearns for a reality that no longer exists ("sueño los cálidos amores del pasado").

Soledad Bianchi says that while the speaker "does not fully reject his present world neither does he decide to accept it blindly" (p. 16). Campos declared in an interview in Chile in July 1986 that if one does not go beyond that initial stage of rejection of the new culture because of profound nostalgia and pain, he closes himself off to what the new culture can offer.[6] But I believe that the speaker of *La ciudad en llamas* does reject the American city and much of the experience it offers. Seen in terms of the speaker's relationships with women, *her* dreams ("tus sueños") are different from his, her past is different (her parents in the swimming pool) and if he remains sufficiently aloof, her *future* and his will be different. Even in the poem in which he says he surrenders to her, he describes himself as a condemned man and her as his prison. He fears that by yielding he will be lost in her dreams and thereby lose some part of himself, and so, the end result is always that *her* dreams, her or their *love*, end up as "cenizas".

The speaker describes how the woman "hides" his luggage ("En el sótano ocultó mi equipaje") and how she suggests they live "in hiding" ("Ella me dijo que aquí viviríamos escondidos"). Living in hiding can suggest the flight of the exile but seems here to refer to acceptance of life in the new space as an escape from (or abandonment of) the memory of (or commitment to) the homeland. The relationship with the woman would separate him from his baggage. A United Nations poster says that a suitcase is not the only thing a refugee brings to his homeland, but this luggage that grows into a train represents all the emotional and spiritual weight of the experiences in the homeland and the separation from it. When it cannot, or the speaker does not want it to, be hidden, the speaker will take his suitcase and leave the woman—symbolically withdrawing from the city and the experience of exile in it, even though he has to continue to be physically present there.

He rejects the reality in which he finds himself—rejects the American city. The speaker of *La ciudad en llamas* is really a lost soul who understands, but, nevertheless, does not totally accept, that he cannot be in his country and must be somewhere else now and perhaps forever. He does not take refuge in trying to recreate here the realities of his own country (that would be another illusion). He confronts his present reality but does not become integrated with it.

Soledad Bianchi says that in both of Campos's books, the speaker is in exile. In *Las últimas fotografías*, a known atmosphere becomes strange because of savagery and violence. In *La ciudad en llamas*, his voice is truly foreign in the American city (pp. 11, 13). In the first, the photographic imagery produces an illusion of objectivity. In the later book, the speaker seems passive, almost an observer at his own life, which contradictorily makes his pain seem more acute. Both books are haunting and the experience of the first is collective; Campos' testimony a product of his own and others' experiences. The speaker of *La ciudad en llamas* seems to have a more personal voice; the experience of exile perhaps ultimately cannot be shared.

Soledad Bianchi closes her introduction to *La ciudad en llamas* with the thought that now that Javier Campos has exorcized in these two books the horror he felt about what has happened in Chile and his experiences in exile, perhaps he can "dream different images and poems," "freer with fewer fears" (p. 18). Campos returned to Chile in the summer of 1986 for the first time since 1977. In the interview mentioned previously, he describes a "short circuit" upon returning to a country which has changed and knowing that he has also changed through the experience of exile. The situation of Chile and that of exile have not changed. The experiences in Chile followed by the return to the space of the American city will certainly begin a new stage in Javier Campos' exile and his poetic expression of it.

Notes

[1] *Tejas verdes* (Esplugas de Llobregat [Barcelona]: Editorial Ariel, 1974. See also: Alejandro Witker, *Prisión en Chile* (México: Fondo de Cultura Económica); Ximena Ortúzar, *Represión y tortura en el cono sur* (México: Extemporáneos, 1977). Some of this discussion of testimonial literature and exile literature is based on conversations with Javier Campos and a radio interview with him in Spring 1986 at California State University, Chico.

[2] "América Latina: Exilio y literatura" (*Cuadernos Americanos*, No. 6, November-December 1984): 7-14.

[3] *Entre la lluvia y el arcoiris: Antología de jóvenes poetas chilenos* [first page says *Entre la lluvia y el arcoiris: Algunos poetas chilenos*] (Rotterdam: Ediciones del Instituto para el Nuevo Chile, 1983). Bianchi includes seventeen poets born between 1943 and 1961. Some, such as Gonzalo Millán, had already published books before 1973, while others' production began later. Bianchi includes a biographical statement—*ars poetica* by each of the poets.

[4] Campos' works include the following **poetry:** *Variaciones sobre distintos temas de las moscas* (I. *Las moscas*, II. *Las banderas y las calles*; fifteen and

eight poems, respectively), a book of poems written between 1970 and 1973 that was to have been published in *Ramona* on 11 September 1986; *Las últimas fotografías* (Montevideo: Acali, 1981); *La ciudad en llamas / The City in Flames* (Concepción, Chile: LAR [Ediciones Literatura Americana Reunida], 1986), introduction by Soledad Bianchi, "Un sonámbulo por los paisajes de sus sueños" / "A Sleepwalker in the Landscapes of His Dreams," pp. 10-19 (all further references will appear in the text), English translation by Irene B. Hodgson; **short stories:** "El dorado mes de septiembre" (*Literatura chilena: creación y crítica*, 23 [1983]: 32-33); "Agua final" (included in "Narrativa chilena reciente" in *Araucaria de Chile* [Madrid], 12 [1980]: 172-174); "El domador de serpientes" (*Paula* [Santiago, Chile], May 1975: 185-188; **articles:** "La joven poesía chilena en el período 1961-1973" (*Cuadernos Hispanoamericanos*, 415 [January 1985]: 128-144); "José Ramírez, *Poesia dell'esilio*" (*Araucaria de Chile* [Madrid], 14 [1981]: 360); "Poesía y proceso revolucionario" (*El diario color* [Concepción, Chile], 2 September 1975: 2).

Some of my information on *Las últimas fotografías* is based on conversations with Campos in the Fall of 1981 and the Spring of 1982. See also Kathleen N. March (also present at many of the conversations with Campos), "Javier Campos y la dialéctica de la poesía del exilio" (9 pp. ms., paper presented at the conference Literature of Hispanic Exile at the University of Missouri—Columbia, 25-27 March 1982) and Aristóbulo Pardo, "*Las últimas fotografías* de Javier Campos" (*Nivel* [*Gaceta de Cultura*], 236 [1982]: 8).

La ciudad en llamas was to have been presented at the Colegio Médico in Concepción when it came out in July of 1986, but the presentation was cancelled at the last minute for political reasons based on negative information received from individuals at the University of Concepción. (The presentation did take place at the Sociedad de Escritores de Chile on 2 September 1986.)

[5] From a 1985 draft of *La ciudad en llamas*.

[6] A misprint in *La ciudad en llamas*, p. 16, says "regret" instead of "reject." Interview with Pacián Martínez, "Javier Campos: 'Me parece muy importante que se reúna a los poetas dispersos' " (Concepción, Chile: *La Gaceta del Sur*, 24 August 1986: 4-5).

NOSTALGIA E IMAGINACION CREADORA EN *TANTAS VECES PEDRO* DE ALFREDO BRYCE ECHENIQUE

Luis Eyzaguirre
University of Connecticut

Ejemplares son los narradores que logran proponer con sus obras universos coherentes consigo mismos y en relación enriquecedora con el mundo de la realidad de la que nacen. Tales son los universos que emergen de la obra de escritores de la estatura de Onetti, Cortázar, García Márquez, Roa Bastos, Carpentier, y tantos otros nombres merecidamente consagrados en la literatura hispanoamericana. Son las suyas creaciones que existen en tensiones constantes con los elementos que las constituyen, pero que, al mismo tiempo, y precisamente por eso, conquistan una totalidad coherente emisora de sentidos múltiples en precaria y genésica permutación.

La obra narrativa, cuento y novela, del peruano Alfredo Bryce Echenique se sitúa ciertamente en este plano totalizador, al que asciende, sin embargo, por caminos diferentes de los transitados por los narradores citados más arriba. Injustamente poco difundida en Hispanoamérica (aparte del Perú, naturalmente), y casi ignorada en Estados Unidos, la obra de Bryce ha atraído entusiastas lectores y bien informados críticos en Francia, donde vivió y enseñó el narrador por varios años, y en España, donde vive en estos momentos. Con una parsimonia que podría contrastar con la aparente desmesura de sus libros mismos, la narrativa de Bryce continúa abriéndose camino en el mundo de la crítica e incrementando el número de sus lectores. Todo de manera tan segura que hace que los espacios conquistados hasta ahora parezcan ya definitivos.

La integridad y coherencia de la obra del narrador peruano empiezan ya a constituirse en 1968 con su primer volumen de cuentos, *Huerto cerrado*. Al carácter fundacional de varios de estos cuentos se suman pronto la novela *Un mundo para Julius* en 1970, *La felicidad, ja, ja*, cuentos de 1974, y en 1977 este original universo narrativo alcanza su completud artística, según yo lo entiendo, con la aparición de la novela *Tantas veces Pedro*. (El título completo es *La Pasión según San Pedro Balbuena que fue Tantas veces Pedro, y que nunca pudo negar a nadie*). En sus dos últimas novelas, *La vida exagerada de Martín Romaña* de 1981, y *El hombre que hablaba de Octavia de Cádiz* de 1985, confirmando lo observado en *Tantas veces Pedro*, se revela una febril actividad memoradora que re-ordena los hechos y propone una nueva versión más amplia y acogedora de ellos. El narrador de los acontecimientos se puede ahora recrear en un mundo de ficción hecho ya familiar, conocedor de sus leyes y consciente de sus límites.

La desafiante morosidad de la narrativa de Bryce es consecuencia, fundamentalmente, de una lenta y progresiva inmersión en un denso mundo de recuerdos. La memoria individual que convoca estos recuerdos se resiste a aceptar el orden, peso y sentido que sugieren los hechos que revisa. A diferencia de la narrativa ya institucionalizada del "boom", que se estructura con frecuencia significativa en base a transcendentales momentos transformadores de la realidad conocida, o en epifánicos momentos de revelación, la narrativa de Bryce se constituye gradualmente como *escritura* recorriendo los laberínticos meandros de una memoria que labora obstinadamente transformando el sentido de los hechos memorados. La heterogeneidad y, a veces, hasta impertinencia de los recuerdos hallan su cauce en las estructuras que la ficción les va creando. Y, así nuevamente organizados, se erigen en el presente de una narración diferente y original.

La *escritura* de Bryce, entendida ésta en términos propuestos por Roland Barthes en *El grado cero de la escritura*, por ejemplo, nace de este compromiso entre el mundo contradictorio de los recuerdos y la libertad de la memoria para re-crearlos. En Bryce, todos los diferentes (y conflictivos) contextos de los que han surgido estos recuerdos confluyen en un tiempo y en un espacio que la memoria ha conquistado. Todo este largo, necesario y, en ocasiones, hasta exasperante diálogo entre recuerdos e imaginación memoradora logra establecer la *escritura* de Bryce Echenique como un *signo total*. Insisto en el término *escritura* por ser el que Bryce mismo aplica a su obra: "Todo intento de esquema fue siempre traicionado por la escritura misma . . . no tengo una concepción de la novela como género literario, tengo simplemente una concepción de la escritura"—dice en una entrevista (*Imagen*, No. 53. Caracas, 27 Jun. - 4 Jul. 1972). Y en 1974, en otra entrevista, agrega: "Además, siendo mi literatura bastante oral, una narración que yo cuento a un presunto lector, mantengo para mí el derecho de alargarla como se alarga a veces una conversación que es buena y agradable. ¿Y la estructura? preguntarán sin duda los más. La verdad es que hasta hoy me interesa poco. Me interesa la *escritura* antes que la estructura. Simplemente poner mi historia oral en papel". Y, más adelante, "Yo creo que siempre hay algo que queda y que, según la necesidad de la propia escritura, aflorará . . . (*Hispamérica*, Año II, No. 6, 1974).

La libertad de la memoria para escoger en el mundo de los recuerdos es sólo momentánea, y no podría prolongarse por el curso de toda una narración, especialmente una tan extensa como la de Bryce. Es aquí donde esta *escritura* entra en correspondencia con el concepto proustiano del tiempo. Proust es una presencia frecuente en la crítica que se ocupa de la obra de Bryce, así como una alusión reiterativa en la narración misma. En varios momentos de *La vida exagerada de Martín Romaña*, por ejemplo, se habla del "loco marcelprousteo" del protagonista. Sin embargo, de manera parecida a cómo la obra de Bryce se aparta de los cánones propuestos por la novela hispanoamericana del "boom", también recoge sólo en parte el legado del autor de *A la búsqueda del tiempo perdido*. Lo que se acepta es la concepción general del tiempo que se desprende reiteradamente de la narración proustiana; esto es, que "el tiempo de que disponemos es elástico; las pasiones que sentimos lo expanden, las que inspiramos lo contraen, y el hábito llena el resto", que es cómo se expresa en uno de muchos momentos de la monumental obra de Proust. Extender, expandir el tiempo para luego detenerlo, y llenar el momento así creado con ansias no realizadas. Es lo que Martín Romaña en *La vida exagerada* . . . y Pedro Balbuena en *Tantas veces Pedro* están afanosamente tratando de hacer. Aparte de estas correspondencias en la concepción general del tiempo en la narración novelesca, hay diferencias claves entre el orden fenomenológico a que adhiere la narración proustiana y la sucesión de recuerdos conflictivos que estructuran la narración de Bryce. Esta diferencia, por cierto central, puede explicar los contrastes entre el *buen tono*, el *buen gusto* y control de la narración de Proust, y la desmesura desafiante en la del narrador hispanoamericano. Como consecuencia de estos desajustes, el mundo cerrado, obsesivo y restrictivo de Proust contrasta con la expansividad e inclusividad del de Bryce.

La lucha de la memoria por crear sus propios espacios empieza en la obra de Bryce con el primer volumen de cuentos, *Huerto cerrado*, donde los protagonistas luchan por asirse a recuerdos que se desintegran. Semejante es la situación en varios de los textos de *La felicidad, ja, ja*. Este primer estadio de la narrativa de Bryce en su camino a la constitución de una escritura coherente y totalizadora es también al que pertenece su novela mejor conocida, *Un mundo para Julius*. En ésta, Julius, protagonista apenas adolescente, no puede con el peso concreto de una realidad que lo abruma y llega al final todavía debatiéndose entre recuerdos que se le complican con lo que él llama "varios niveles" de la realidad. Sin poder transformar los hechos de una infancia donde apariencias y realidades no se conjugan, Julius vive siempre bajo "esa amenaza de pena que ya es tristeza", que es cómo se expresa al final de la novela. Toda la vida vivida hasta ese momento culmina en "un vacío grande, hondo, oscuro. "Y—concluye la novela—Julius no tuvo más remedio que llenarlo con un llanto largo y silencioso, llenecito de preguntas, eso sí". Hasta este momento no hay reconciliación en la obra de Bryce entre lo que el protagonista llama "varios niveles". Ni en el mundo de la realidad, ni en el de la memoria.

En *La felicidad, ja, ja,* junto a cuentos en los que el mundo de los recuerdos aún no encuentra un orden nuevo, resaltan ya textos donde el personaje puede reestructurar en el mundo de la memoria las experiencias vividas. El tiempo se expande y los espacios se amplían en el mundo de los recuerdos y éstos entonces pueden proponer nuevos sentidos cuando se los memora. Así el protagonista "arma", "compone" la realidad, ahora *su* realidad, suavizadas las aristas más toscas y conflictivas. No importa que esta nueva realidad "armada" por la memoria haya sido elaborada con un mucho de recuerdos y sólo con un algo de realidad vivida.

En *Muerte de Sevilla en Madrid*, uno de los cuentos más notables de Bryce, y de la cuentística hispanoamericana, Sevilla, uno de los tantos personajes marginados de Bryce, consigue insertar toda la vida no vivida en sólo un momento que se pudiera denominar "momento proustiano". Es aquél creado por el recuerdo de la amistad que le otorgara Salvador Escalante, ser excepcional. El texto insiste en la precariedad de ese momento hecho sólo de ilusiones irrealizables. Sin embargo, la omnipresencia de ese recuerdo regenerador posibilita la transmutación del fin patético de Sevilla en la ciudad de Madrid en un momento de apoteosis privada. El salto suicida de Sevilla por la ventana de su hotel se transforma, por la fuerza del recuerdo, en un salto hacia el encuentro definitivo con Salvador Escalante en el espacio creado por la naciente imaginación del alienado protagonista.

El paso siguiente en la narrativa de Bryce se da, primero, en el cuento "Antes de la cita con los Linares", de *La felicidad, ja, ja*, y se afirma, luego, en la novela *Tantas veces Pedro*. En el cuento, el protagonista, mientras espera al matrimonio Linares, los amigos que mejor le conocen, pasa revisión a los datos más significativos de su vida. Se adentra en el espeso mundo de sus recuerdos, reconquista para ellos un nuevo espacio en un nuevo tiempo, y, reorganizados, los inserta en este recién creado tiempo extendido de una ficción literaria. Todo este proceso, estimulado por la anunciada llegada del los Linares, tiene lugar mientras los espera. Y, así entonces, cuando ellos llegan, puede ofrecerles el producto terminado, en el que tanto los Linares como el protagonista y el momento mismo que viven han sido ya ficcionalizados.

> —¿Y esto qué es, Sebastián?—pregunta su amigo.
> —Ah, un cuento; me puse a escribir mientras los esperaba; . . .
> . . . .
> —¿Y el título?
> —Aún no lo sé; había pensado llamarlo "Doctor psiquiatra", pero dadas las circunstancias, creo que le voy a poner "Antes de la cita, con ustedes, con los Linares."

Tantas veces Pedro, la novela que nos ocupa en particular, ya participa plenamente de esta transformación de la realidad de los recuerdos en la realidad de la ficción. La historia que se lee en la novela es la misma en la que Pedro Balbuena, su protagonista, puede verse "personaje de una historia maravillosa que nunca recuperaré—dice Pedro—y que tal vez nunca lograré escribir porque de pronto fui expulsado de ella, de mi propia historia, y me quedé sin todo lo que me faltaba. . .". El personaje expulsado se refiere, claro está, a una "historia maravillosa" que conformaría un "libro imposible" que enlazaría todas sus vidas posibles. Un libro siempre "por escribir", dice en otro lugar, mientras está, en verdad, constantemente siendo escrito. Un "libro imposible—puntualiza—porque no se termina ni siquiera cuando lo vuelvo a cerrar". Un libro autóctono, siempre escribiéndose.

Se podrían citar varios ejemplos de momentos en que se observa el paso de la "realidad" de la vida de Pedro Balbuena a la "realidad" de la escritura. En el centro de esas fisuras está siempre Sophie, la mujer inalcanzable, el objeto amoroso. Sophie de la realidad, si es que de veras existió, es, desde luego, diferente de las varias Sophies que Pedro "arma" con los recuerdos. Pedro se crea muchos, innumerables mitos sobre las posibles e imaginadas Sophies, y en todos ellos llega él a creer. Para todas las varias formas que puede tomar la mujer que motiva la escritura, Pedro encuentra los modos de representar estas formas. Así, al principio, cree ver a Sophie en la estudiante de California con quien viaja a París. Cuando los gestos, palabras y acciones de la muchacha no corresponden a los que serían de Sophie, Pedro se aleja de la realidad del momento y se mete en la de los recuerdos. Ya no estaría con esta mujer de California en París sino con Sophie en Venecia. Y ahora sí que son auténticas las reacciones de esta imaginada Sophie frente a las muchas excentricidades de Pedro. Por eso dice a su acompañante, expulsándola del momento: "No me interrumpas, por favor, estoy escribiendo". Y ya inmerso en el mundo de los recuerdos, imagina toda una complicada red de situaciones que llegan a parecer más reales que la realidad misma. Luego de un largo rato en que se lee la situación imaginada, la mujer lo interrumpe cuando se da cuenta que Pedro ha dejado de escribir y está repitiendo la frase que se convierte en el leit-motif de sus frustradas relaciones con Sophie: "tres meses, cinco días, y las últimas veinticuatro horas que fueron atroces". El fluir de los recuerdos se ha roto y el protagonista se ha quedado también fuera de la ficción y fuera de la realidad. Alienado de la vida y la literatura, sólo puede repetir mecánicamente el fin de la aventura con Sophie.

Más adelante está Claudine con la que comparte episodios increíbles de los que también se propone una version ficcionalizada. Muy al final está Beatriz/Beatrice con cuyo nombre Pedro se recrea en su repetición: "Beatrice de nombre, y de factura Boticelli". Con ella cree Pedro haber alcanzado algún tipo de destino: "Por primera vez en su vida, Pedro sintió que la vida no pasaba en vano", dice el texto. Hasta la misma semejanza física de la Beatrice de este episodio con la Sophie de los recuerdos hace este encuentro mucho más peligroso que los demás. A veces, las dos se confunden tanto en la vida de Pedro como en lo que éste escribe. Por eso, cuando se produce la ruptura con Beatrice, ya sólo le queda la Sophie de un recuerdo desgastado por las reiteradas convocaciones. La realidad del objeto amoroso se desdibuja aún más en una última aventura con una Sophie (muy posiblemente la incitadora de los muchos recuerdos) que le cuenta al hombre con quien viaja cuán maravilloso es que Pedro se acuerde de un encuentro de hace quince años: "¡Qué bárbaro!—dice esta Sophie. Es como una máquina loca de recordar. Ha vivido tanto para mí, te cuenta tales cosas que por momentos parece que siempre hubiera estado contigo . . . No sé cómo decirte . . . conmigo".

Agotado, Pedro, personaje de su propia ficción, decide poner fin al libro, que, dejado a su suerte, podría haber seguido proliferando hasta un infinito. Para terminar una historia que hubiera querido dejar en suspenso, debe sacar de ella a Sophie. Lo consigue "fingiendo morir" y, mientras él "muere", hace que ella confiese haber vivido en la realidad hechos que habían ocurrido sólo en la ficción. Sólo entonces, cuando Sophie "se sale del libro", la historia puede terminar. *Sin ella* no puede haber historia, así como *con ella* en él el libro no podría concluir. Y en un epílogo, como en una venganza postrera, una última Sophie le arranca de las manos a Pedro un texto, supuesto generador de toda esta ficción, y deja que su perro termine de destrozarlo. El libro que se acaba de leer, *Tantas veces Pedro*, podría haber quedado así no contado.

Todo lo expuesto o sugerido en las páginas anteriores debiera señalar cómo la obra narrativa de Alfredo Bryce Echenique se estructura fuera de los cánones ya convencionales de la ficción hispanoamericana de los últimos años. Crea sus propios cánones en una prolija serie de *encuentros* y *desencuentros* del mundo de la memoria del sujeto con una realidad elusiva. Hay, a veces, confluencia de deseos y realidad, momentos en que el siempre necesario lector-interlocutor quisiera ser incluido. Otras veces, las más, hay rechazo de los deseos por una realidad restrictiva. Este sistema de relaciones se instaura en la obra de Bryce a lo largo de un dificultoso proceso que le da unidad y coherencia. Coherente con su todo y coherente con sus partes. Es así cómo podría incluso postularse que la vida desmesurada y conflictiva de Pedro Balbuena en *Tantas veces Pedro* tiene sus raíces más profundas y definitorias en ese lejano mundo vacuo que sus mayores legaran al niño Julius de la primera novela de Bryce, *Un mundo para Julius*. Ese mundo vacuo con el que luchaba Julius, hecho de "zonas donde los afectos se diluían".

LA (IM)POSIBILIDAD DE (RE)INTEGRARSE: COTEJO TEMATICO EN DOS NOVELAS DE A. YAÑEZ Y A. CARPENTIER

Lourdes Rojas
Colgate University

Agustín Yáñez y Alejo Carpentier publican respectivamente y con seis años de diferencia entre ellas, las novelas *La creación* (1959) y *Los pasos perdidos* (1953)[1]

Además de la cercanía en la fecha de su aparición, las novelas en cuestión, muestran coincidencias significativas en el relato que justifican su estudio conjunto. Nos referimos no sólo a coincidencias temáticas: el conflicto del artista (músico) y su creación en un mundo alienante, sino también a coincidencias en la composición de los textos: el viaje como motivo estructurante, el desarraigo del protagonista y su vuelta a las raíces. Y también la creación de estereotipos femeninos, que aunque variados en su forma, resultan monótonos en su significado: son vehículos que mediatizan la relación protagonista-mundo.

En *La creación*, los personajes femeninos: María, Victoria y Pandora son intérpretes de mundo para Gabriel. Las tres, aunque de distinta manera y en etapas diferentes, le ayudan en su intento de plasmar en las creaciones musicales sus vivencias más auténticas. Las tres son creaciones "mestizas" de mito y realidad, promesas de infinito que le permiten al protagonista intentar un re-encuentro con sus raíces. Digo *intentar,* porque el protagonista no logra entrar en ese espacio absoluto que desidera, y termina tomando conciencia de su precariedad: de la imposibilidad de sumergirse en ese espacio deseado. En *Los pasos perdidos* de Carpentier los personajes femeninos funcionan como vehículos de la desmitificación total de la visión de mundo de la obra. De acuerdo con, una premisa que defiende Roberto González Echevarría, en la novela de Carpentier, el protagonista se despoja de la mitificación romántica del reencuentro con los orígenes y del acceso a lo absoluto a través del arte:

> If the protagonist's journey is a Bildungsreise in the Romantic tradition, the culmination of his education is recognizing the necessity of subverting that tradition; restitution, reintegration is impossible, only a plurality-in-the-present.[2]

De igual manera, añado, le resulta imposible al protagonista su reintegración o re-inserción en el espacio salvador del Valle del tiempo detenido a través de su relación con Rosario. Ella, quien le sirve inicialmente de puente con ese mundo, le cierra al final la entrada: Rosario sale encinta y se hace mujer de Marcos; y lo mismo que las señales en el árbol son cubiertas por las aguas, los peldaños del camino de vuelta están perdidos.

El protagonista de ambas novelas busca recuperar su historia total a través de su relación con las mujeres. No con ellas mismas, sino por lo que transparentan. Ellas le brindan el idioma del espacio-tiempo en que él quiere ubicarse y hallarse.

Aunque existe variedad en las diversas concretizaciones de la reintegración del protagonista en ambos textos, hay también un patrón único en el desarrollo general de esta temática en las novelas. De ahí que resulte válido analizar cómo se plasma la temática del retorno en un ejemplo particular en cada texto narrativo, para intentar elucidar la totalidad del proceso.

El primer modelo es la relación Gabriel-Victoria en *La creación* de Agustín Yáñez. Gabriel, músico y compositor regresa después de varios años en Europa a su México natal. Su actitud inicial es conflictiva: de deseo y de rechazo del re-encuentro con su tierra y con las dos mujeres más importantes en su vida hasta entonces: María y Victoria.

Gabriel comienza gradualmente a adentrarse en sus recuerdos de Victoria; a partir de la contemplación de la réplica de la Victoria de Samotracia (presente narrativo), se remonta a un "momento sublime" anterior, la contemplación del original de la obra de arte, que su vez le retrotrae al "momento sublime" inicial: la escena de Victoria en el campanario (raconto). Todo el recuerdo se conjuga y encuentra significado en su experiencia con Victoria y las campanas. La contemplación del original de la Victoria de Samotracia es sublime en tanto y en cuanto le hace revivir el encuentro primero con Victoria: "aquel otro instante decisivo". (p. 63)

La imágenes que describen a Victoria son de fuerza, cambio, movimiento, fugacidad y luz: "caída como centella, presencia del cielo fulminante, alucinante, viento arrasador, fuego, criatura marina..." (p. 57)

Estas imágenes son generalmente asociadas con las fuerzas de la naturaleza. Por una parte son imágenes de la tierra: centella, fuego, viento, mar (elementos deseados esenciales) y a la vez son posibles fuerzas destructoras (elementos temidos, no-deseados).

Sobre la imagen de la mujer-tierra y sus poderes mágicos, Beatrice Tobin señala en su artículo sobre los mitos del poder femenino, que esta analogía (entre la mujer y la tierra como fuente de vida) siempre ha sido motivo de inspiración literaria: "From the very earliest ages of human history, the magical force and wonder of the female was as much marvel as the universe itself".[3] Y ello contribuye a esa ambivalencia que puede sentir el hombre hacia la mujer, como ser deseado y temido, ya que, continúa Tobin en el mismo artículo:

> Woman is worshipped and respected but feared for her greater proximity to the mysterious scheme of things. Her body shared the moon's periodic cycles, the earth's productive powers. Thus she was part of that nature which he could not control and which could destroy him at whim.[4]

Reacción similar de ambivalencia provocará Victoria en Gabriel desde el momento de su primer encuentro y a lo largo de su relación: deseo (atracción por lo maravilloso) y rechazo (temor de perder su libertad, de anularse en su entrega).

Al concebir a Victoria, como *La Mujer*, Gabriel comienza su relación con ella transponiendo los valores de *una mujer* (nivel real, concreto) al plano de las esencias (nivel mítico, indefinido): *La mujer*. Victoria participará cada vez más de este último nivel y se transformará poco a poco hasta convertirse en la esencia misma de la Belleza, "estrellastral: Victoria, o la suma de todas las mujeres". (p. 265)

La escena en cuestión es enormemente simbólica: es un doble rito iniciático de revelación y de ascensión. Al revivir en la evocación esta escena en *La creación*, Gabriel intenta "volver" a la torre a través de su "re-encuentro" con Victoria. Es un intento de apresar su pasada vivencia ritual: su rito de iniciación en el *amor* y en el *arte*, con y por *la mujer*. En ello busca Gabriel el vínculo que lo restituirá a su pueblo, a su raíz, a lo esencial y primigíneo, a su verdadera voz.

Otra función de Victoria es la de elemento *transformador*. La presencia de Victoria transforma en un instante la vida del protagonista. La belleza de Victoria es la que produce el salto cualitativo de Gabriel de un plano inferior a otro superior—de *adolescente* le convierte en *hombre*, de *campanero* en *músico*. Tal transformación ocurre, porque la belleza de la mujer provoca el sentimiento del amor, (o la conciencia de ese sentimiento) en el joven. Así, la función de Victoria en la vida de Gabriel, desde sus comienzos, va a estar íntimamente vinculada con las nociones de Belleza, Amor y creación artística. Esta función transformadora e inspiracional de la belleza de Victoria remite al concepto platónico de belleza.

El período histórico que cubre *La creación*, la segunda década del siglo XX, constituye una etapa de renacimiento en la vida intelectual y artística mexicanas. Como señala John Flasher en su *México contemporáneo en las novelas de A. Yáñez*, Vasconcelos le dio una enorme importancia a las distintas manifestaciones de la cultura en México.[5] Los *Diálogos de Platón* fueron publicados y difundidos bajo su dirección como Ministro de Educación. Esta es la obra que lee Gabriel al volver a México y en la que basa su composición musical más ambiciosa.

El deseo de buscar a Victoria—después de la separación de Europa—surge en Gabriel a partir de la lectura de los *Diálogos* de Platón, específicamente del *Banquete*:

> Llegó a mi destierro el primer volumen de los *Diálogos* platónicos editados por un Vasconcelos . . . me transportaron a un mundo antes insospechado: el juicio, . . . el alma, la santidad, . . . la belleza, el amor . . . (p. 118)

La importancia del sentido de la vista en la experiencia de la belleza es otro elemento platónico, que aparece en *La creación*. En la escena final con Victoria, esta importancia de la vista se hace más evidente en la descripción de la belleza translúcida y esencial de Victoria; donde los ojos son verdadero reflejo del alma:

> . . . la llama en los ojos de la inválida reverberaba con esplendor de luz a punto de apagarse. Nunca brillaron así, tanto, aquellos ojos—vida, dulzura y esperanza—en las cavadas cuencas, por donde la fuerza del alma derramaba gozosa claridad . . . En los ojos metálicos brillaba la eterna luz. (p. 307)

La descripción platónica de la Belleza, se conjuga con una concepción cristiana de la imagen de Victoria, encarnada en la mater Dolorosa. Frente a Ella, Gabriel se prosterna, como ante la imagen de la Virgen doliente: "Gabriel se prosternó . . . El retablo de la Anunciación se trocaba en el duelo angélico de la Solead". (p. 302)

El simbolismo religioso de Victoria es evidente en los calificativos que le da Gabriel en esta escena del encuentro final: "Mater dolorosa", "Gran Señora misericordiosa", "la doliente", "la siempre piadosa", "la siempre propicia" . . . y además, su función de madre redentora, que perdona los descarríos del "hijo pródigo", la colocan definitivamente dentro del marco de ese concepto cristiano.

Victoria como Beatriz busca alejarse de la belleza temporal de los sentidos, e inmortalizarse con las cualidades supernaturales de la "donna angelicata". Este elemento cristianizante de la Belleza es para Gabriel la otra parte de la síntesis buscada y a la que finalmente llega en esta escena: la mezcla de lo pagano y lo cristiano. Para Gabriel, Victoria se ubica en el cruce de una diosa pagana (La Victoria de Samotracia) y una "donna angelicata" (la Beatriz de Dante); ambas son caras de una misma moneda, y cumplen igual función mediadora entre el artista y su afán de reinserción al mundo. Con ambos aspectos se relaciona Gabriel en su relación amorosa, de la cual finalmente se aleja él mismo, consciente de su precariedad. Con Victoria y por Victoria, Gabriel ve aunque fugazmente una posible reintegración, pero es por ella precisamente que él se da cuenta de la imposibilidad de su re-inserción. La fugacidad del instante maravilloso denuncia la permanencia de su cotidiano mundo de sombras. Ha sido una experiencia enriquecedora, pero no solucionadora de su conflicto básico.

Al igual que en *La creación* de A. Yáñez, el protagonista de *Los pasos perdidos* es el hijo pródigo que ha regresado al hogar donde encuetra los eslabones que establecen el vínculo con su infancia: el idioma, y la mujer. Ambos protagonistas son músicos en busca de su realización en la auténtica creación artística que esperan lograr en contacto con sus raíces, con su historia. Sin embargo, hay una diferencia esencial en los dos regresos: Gabriel en *La creación* vuelve a México con esa esperanza de realización; el protagonista de *Los pasos perdidos* empieza a descubrir esa posibilidad al tomar contacto con el suelo americano. El pasado es para Gabriel la forma de entender su presente y su futuro. Para el protagonista sin nombre de *Los pasos perdidos*, el pasado y el presente coexisten, se dan superpuestos y en su relación, en su cotejo, se da el vértice donde él desea ubicarse.

Rosario es la última figura femenina con quien entabla una relación imporante el protagonista-narrador de *Los pasos perdidos*. Ella surge en su vida en un momento clave de su viaje ya en el Nuevo Mundo; cuando él ha decidido internarse en la selva en busca de los instrumentos musicales. Esta es la etapa más importante del viaje como vehículo de la búsqueda, de la aventura.

El encuentro con Rosario es el encuentro con un nuevo espacio: con la selva americana. La descripción física de la mujer es síntesis del medio. La característica sobresaliente de ella es la del Nuevo Mundo: su mestizaje.

Este encuentro con Rosario está marcado además por una mutua sensación de reconocimiento. En cuanto a Rosario, el reconocimiento se da en la mirada que ella le dirige: "Me miró como si le fuese conocido" (p. 65). Además, con su apoyo ella vuelve en sí, revive: "La mujer pareció despertar repentinamente: dio un grito y se agarró de mí" (p. 65).

Para el protagonista empieza a partir de aquí un proceso de redescubrimiento de olores, sabores, sonidos y hábitos que creía olvidados. Ejemplo de ello es la recuperación de la facultad de dormir a cualquier hora que tenía de adolescente, y el recuerdo de la compañerita de sus juegos infantiles: María del Carmen, que le trae el olor de las hierbas silvestres que le da Rosario en la posada.

En ese proceso de volver a encontrarse consigo mismo y con el mundo de su infancia, con la vuelta a sus raíces, el protagonista va a contar con y a depender de Rosario, quien va a configurar para él una posibilidad de re-inserción en el mundo primario en el Valle del tiempo detenido, y a la vez será ella quien deshará esa misma posibilidad. La función de Rosario va a ser mediatizar la relación protagonista-Nuevo Mundo, en su doble facultad de puente y abismo. Si el nombre Rosario sugiere mediación, la asociación Rosario-agua es motivo estructurante de su papel doble: como las aguas Rosario *descrea,* disuelve, destruye.

El protagonista-narrador comienza a sentir la presencia de Rosario a través del elemento en que se realizará más claramente su función de mediatriz, de guía del protagonista en su entrada a la selva: el agua. Rosario aparece en una altura, rodeada de un paisaje de nubes, de niebla, en un puente de piedra sobre un torrente hondo, cuyas aguas sonaban atronadoras: nube, niebla, río, todas son configuraciones acuosas.

De gran importancia resulta la presencia de otro elemento natural: el fuego, asociado a la percepción de la mujer. Si con el agua Rosario cumple función similar (crea y destruye) con el fuego también se subraya su doble papel mediador. El fuego, en proceso más rápido que el agua, también transforma, destruyendo y dando forma a los elementos que toca. Sobre esta característica del fuego Gaston Bachelard señala:

> El fuego, para el hombre que contempla, es un ejemplo, a la vez, de transformación rápida y circunstancial. Menos monótono y abstracto que el agua corriente, . . . el fuego sugiere el anhelo de cambiar, de atropellar al tiempo . . . [6]

Junto al fuego y por su acción rápida y transformacional, Rosario adquiere una nueva dimensión, al revelársele al protagonista el encanto de su persona y el atractivo de su belleza.

El encuentro sexual con Rosario en la cabaña marca el fin de lo anterior y el comienzo de una nueva forma de vida para el protagonista. El sexo es comunión y apertura, es puerta que le abrirá al protagonista la entrada a la selva: ". . . Como si los cuerpos hubieran sellado un pacto que fuera el comienzo de un nuevo modo de vivir" (p. 121).

El protagonista también siente la importancia del encuentro, que es posesión, en contraste con Ruth y Mouche (sus mujeres anteriores) a quienes no poseía. Con Rosario se instala como dueño: "Me he *sembrado* bajo el vellón que acaricio con mano de *amo*, y mi gesto cierra una gozosa confluencia de sangres que se encontraron" (p. 122) (subrayado nuestro).

El verbo "sembrarse" tiene también la connotación de semilla, lo cual evoca la idea de germinación, comienzo, origen de un proceso. Desde este punto de vista el protagonista alude a su renacer por el sexo o a través de la relación sexual con Rosario; "el vellón" es la tierra fértil en la que él fructificará como una semilla, la relación en que encontrará un nuevo modo de vivir.

Si por un lado el protagonista entiende el amor, en parte, como posesión sexual; Rosario, por otro lado, entiende su relación en términos de servidumbre. Rosario al servirle hace dos cosas para el protagonista: primeramente le incorpora al grupo, haciéndole sentirse igual que los otros hombres que les rodean: siguen los códigos de la relación entre los sexos del lugar que habitan. Segundo, ella le crea un espacio: le da su función en el grupo, y lo que es más importante, una definición de ser hombre, una nueva identidad de varón: el que posee una hembra que le sirve. Rosario literal y metafóricamente le hace su casa al protagonista, le da su espacio en su cuerpo (con el sexo) y en el grupo social (con su actitud).

Con la penetración de Rosario empieza el protagonista su penetración de la selva. El lenguaje que él usa para describir su entrada en la selva está cargado de alusiones sexuales que justifican la anterior asociación. La entrada es descrita como una puerta señalada por tres letras V superpuestas (la imagen gráfica recuerda la apertura vaginal) en la corteza de un tronco y el proceso todo es una "penetración", un "introducirse" en *túneles* angostos: " . . . una señal semejante a las tres letras V superpuestas verticalmente, . . . una penetraba dentro de la otra, . . . un pasadizo abovedado, . . . estrecho . . . meter la curiara . . . que se introdujo en este angosto túnel . . . " (p. 128).

De la misma manera que Rosario le sirve de puente al protagonista en su viaje por la selva, ella le va a servir de abismo, al cortarle el vínculo con el mundo de Santa Mónica de los Venados. Para Rosario, la condición necesaria para asegurarse la buena conducta del varón es la unión libre, sin contratos legales. Para ella, casarse es "caer bajo el peso de las leyes que hicieron los hombre y no las mujeres" (p. 179). Mientras Rosario al unirse con el protagonista tenía conciencia de su compromiso, para él la ausencia del vínculo legal es evidencia de la precariedad de la unión.

Cuando intenta volver una segunda vez, el protagonista no puede rehacer los vínculos rotos. El sitio es diferente. La choza en que hiciera el amor por primera vez con Rosario ha sido destruida por la vegetación. Las lluvias han producido la crecida del río y es imposible encontrar el tronco de las tres V superpuestas. Rosario tampoco es la misma: "es mujer de Marcos y está preñada recién" (p. 219).

Si la búsqueda del protagonista termina en un fracaso; por otro lado, la experiencia le ha brindado el conocimiento de lo que es: un compositor musical que ha podido crear, oír su propia voz en las composiciones musicales que escribe en Santa Mónica de los Venados. Y en ello sí se ha cambiado.

La búsqueda de ambos viajes es básicamente una preocupación por las esencias (la vuelta a los orígenes). Yáñez y Carpentier muestran en estas obras, una voluntad de capturar la esencia que se desvanece. El espacio que se configura como una superrealidad necesaria, donde las limitaciones de lo real no se den; surge en un proceso doble y complementario de creación y descreación, que gira en torno a un personaje femenino.

La desromantización que sufre la vuelta a los orígenes, tiñe igualmente la función de los personajes femeninos en el texto. En un último análisis, las creaciones de los protagonistas son ilusión; de la misma manera el regreso en el tiempo es también ilusión: ni Gabriel encontrará de nuevo la experiencia sublime del campanario (Victoria-Beatrice), ni el protagonista de *Los pasos perdidos* logrará re-integrarse a sus orígenes (Rosario-María del Carmen).

Notas

[1] Agustín Yáñez, *La creación* (México: Fondo de Cultura Económica, 1959). Alejo Carpentier, *Los pasos perdidos* (Chile: Editorial Orbe, 1970). Para citas y numeración de página, en adelante incorporadas al texto, usaré estas ediciones.

[2] Roberto González Echevarría, *The Pilgrim at Home* (Ithaca: Cornell University Press, 1977) p. 164.

[3] Beatrice Tobin, "Images of Women: Myths and Stereotypes", en *Una historia de servicio. Edición conmemorativa del 66 aniversario* (Puerto Rico: Universidad Interamericana, 1979), p. 118.

[4] Tobin, p. 119.

[5] John Flasher, *México contemporáneo en las novelas de Agustín Yáñez* (México: Editorial Porrúa, 1969), p. 109.

[6] Gaston Bachelard, *Psicoanálisis del fuego* (Argentina: Schapire Editor, 1973), p. 37.

THE DYNAMIC OF MEMORY AND IMAGINATION IN *LA CASA DE LOS ESPIRITUS* by ISABEL ALLENDE

Colleen Kattau Craven
Syracuse University

Written in exile, Isabel Allende's novel, *La casa de los espíritus* spans three matrilineal generations (and one generation unborn) of a family which by all indication is part of the ruling faction of Chile's middle class.[1] The similarities between events in the novel and the historical past of Chile are both startlingly clear yet transformed through the retrospective vantage point of those who have experienced these events and now retain them only at a distance in time and space. The dual meaning of "la historia" becomes an integral element of this "magically real" novel as Allende's characters recall Chile's past and their relation to it. Allende presents these "recuerdos" in a complex, non-linear manner emphasizing the role of imagination and history in forming them. Of course, it would be another paper entirely to specifically address how the novelic images evoke remembrance of actual people and events in Chile's history. I would like to discuss here the dynamic connection between memory and imagination, focusing first on the subjectivity of memory and later on memory as a foundation for the future.

Much of *La casa de los espíritus*[2] is written in the imperfect past tense, as one would use to describe and retell a tale. The reader discovers that there are two very distinct speaking voices interspersed throughout the book. Beginning with Alba, the granddaughter in the Trueba family followed by her grandfather Esteban Trueba, the perspective on the past shifts back and forth giving the reader at times conflicting interpretations of the same events. I do not believe that it is Allende's intent to demonstrate through this technique that remembrance is relative, but rather that many voices must be heard in order to validate history. While reading Alba's account, the "yo" is barely perceptible save for the personalized epilogue and the very first lines of the novel when she acknowledges the guidance given to her by her grandmother Clara, who, as a child was described in the following way:

> . . . ya tenía entonces el hábito de escribir las cosas importantes . . . sin saber que cinquenta años después sus cuadernos me sirvieron para rescatar la memoria del pasado y para sobrevivir a mi propio espanto. (9)

Alba maintains a third person perspective in using these writings to reclaim the past through story telling. Hers becomes the more all-encompassing viewpoint as the reader understands the story's unfolding at ground level. This perspective reflects the self-awareness that she is but one among many personalities interacting to make history—that she is very much a product of her past and thus strongly connected to her mother Blanca and her grandmother Clara as well as to others. Even her name was chosen because "es el último de una cadena de palabras que quieren decir lo mismo." (233) Alba as author continually stresses the extent to which these women give her the strength to survive, both while living and through memory of them. She can keep her sanity and sustain identity with this knowledge of family.

While Alba's version of recorded memory can be considered *collective*, Esteban Trueba's account is autobiographical in nature. His subjective and ego-centered recollections mirror the fact that he has been a powerful individual as both "patrón de un fundo" and as a political personality. His focus is conservative and narrow in describing remembered reality and underscores the unself-critical view he has of himself and his power over "los inquilinos". He says:

> Nadie me va a quitar de la cabeza la idea de que he sido un buen patrón: qualquiera que hubiera visto Las Tres Marías en los tiempos del abandono y la viera ahora, que es un fundo modelo, tendría que estar de acuerdo conmigo . . . Yo era como un padre para ellos . . . con la reforma agraria nos jodimos todos. (53)

Later he asserts, "El día que no podamos echar el guante a las urnas antes que cuenten los votos, nos vamos al carajo." (271)

These are two among many assertions whereby Trueba sums up reality only as he sees it. He relies on a memory separated from the dynamic of history so that if there is no precedent of an event, then in his mind, it will not happen. For instance, he does not understand nor believe Clara's clairvoyant prediction of the powerful earthquake that will destroy so much of Chile or of the bloody coup that will qualitatively change the country's course indefinitely. His unyielding adherence to the status quo of power relations "sin sospechar" will ultimately lead to the destruction of his falsely defined world nearly to the point of losing his beloved granddaughter—the only love that is left to him. Trueba, however, is by no means a one dimensional character. It is his idea in fact to gather all the family's memoirs to form a cohesive chronicle. As he tells Alba, "así podrás llevarte las raíces contigo si algún día tienes que irte de aquí, hijita."(378) He too is influenced by the memory of Clara and Rosa, but the memory remains static and nostalgic and wholly separated from time. Lacking the imaginative capacity to anticipate certain inevitable changes, Trueba remains locked into the past while his world, like an earthquake, will collapse before him.

In contrast, it can be argued that it is the women of the family who, through imagination and memory, are building a foundation for their own survival and for future generations. Before expanding on this point, it is necessary to keep in mind that memory itself has been explained by different systems at diverse moments in history. The novel's emphasis on imagination and the capacity to remember, for example coincides with Classical and Renaissance views of memory. Francis Yates, in her book, *The Art of Memory*,[3] shows how imagination and later magic became integral parts of this art. One aspect of the Classical view for instance, strove to improve memory "by arousing emotional affects through . . . striking and unusual images, beautiful or hideous, comic or obscene."[4] Extending this approach, Aquinas asserted that fantasy and memory were in the same part of the soul. Yates also explains how Bruno, the Renaissance philosopher, tried to develop a memory system based on magic and astrology for he believed that one's power of imagination was the means by which understanding could ultimately be achieved: "To understand is to speculate with images and the understanding is either the 'fantasy or does not exist without it.' "[5]

Interconnections abound among memory, magic, and imagination in *La casa de los espíritus*. The title itself suggests this interplay whereby the house is a holding place of memory and "spirits" from the past continue to exert influence upon the living. More conceretely, the three generations of women rely on their imaginations and their interconnectedness to each other to give them a certain flexibility to see the importance of memory and to know it as a process of continual change. They give individual expression to their recollections, for example, not only orally and through writing (though these are the major means) but also through a specific medium of art:

> A lo largo de los años, Alba fue llenando . . . las . . . murallas de su dormitorio con un inmenso fresco, donde, en medio de una flora venesiana y una fauna imposible de bestias inventadas,

como las que bordaba Rosa en su mantel y cocinaba Blanca en su horno de cerámica, aparecieron los deseos los recuerdos, las tristezas, y las alegrías de su niñez. (240)

The alternative ways of expressing remembrance give space to that which is too difficult or too unclear at the moment to be told through language. Like grafitti on war torn walls or painted murals in Latin America, this personal creativity lends itself to self-reflection and gives meaning and cohesiveness to memory while providing an individual testimony for others to interpret as well. It is not necessarily the memories per se which the three generations all share, but rather the imagination and corresponding creativity going hand in hand with memory which unite them in a common bond. We know for instance that Clara has an uncanny ability to remember the bizarre "cuentos del tío Marcos" (recalling them precisely *because* of their strangeness), and "tenía la desbordante imaginación que heredaron todas las mujeres de su familia por vía materna." (9) Clara can remember because she can project herself into the fantasy of these stories which are experienced through an *active* mental exercise. She can thus retain them almost as if she had lived them herself. Later on, Alba will learn these tales transformed by the "mala memoria" of her mother Blanca, so that damsels become the slayers of dragons and it is the prince who sleeps for one hundred years. These stories will remain as part of the family tradition modified only by the necessities of time and individual imagination. Prompted by the desire to know them always, Alba writes these and other important events just as her grandmother did before in defiance of a faulty memory.

Yates also clarifies *Dante's Inferno* as a kind of "memory system for memorizing"[6] in the classical tradition because essentially Dante descends into a Hell composed of ordered circles categorized according to the severity of the sin. Furthermore, Dante uses symbolic images, allegories, and real personalities of his day and in the past to represent some aspect of wrong-doing, thus systematizing moral reminders of the nature of evil. Just as *Dante's Inferno* begins when Dante finds himself somehow in a "dark wood" on Holy Thursday, so too does Allende begin her novel on this very same day. In the first paragraph we learn that "El día que llegó Barrabás era Jueves Santo." (9) Barrabás is Clara's huge canine pet that ironically shows similar sexual behavior to that of Esteban Trueba, i.e., raping the female victim and leaving her half-dead. (Indeed the day Clara and Trueba marry, Barrabás dies.) The bizarre image of the beast serves as a point of departure for recalling the darker side of the past just as the memory system of Classical Antiquity advocated the use of the odd to evoke and enhance memory. The ignorant beast is like an omen of the "dark wood", or, as Allende describes it, "el terror" in which Chile will find itself when the dictatorship will try to strip memory from the minds of the people.

The bright image of remembrance, in contrast, is Rosa, Clara's older sister and Esteban's first love. She is a beautiful oddity of nature born with yellow eyes and green hair. Like a fragile "ángel de la esperanza" it is understood that she is not long for this world. Rosa's symbolic role as a vision of lost hope for Chile is underscored when Esteban robs her grave. His memory deludes him into believing that she is as beautiful in death as in life:

> Vi a Rosa . . . su imperturbable belleza, tal como la viera muchos años antes . . . me quedé mirándola fascinado . . . una brisa avanzó . . . y en un instante la novia inmutable se deshizo como un encantamiento, se desintegró en un polvillo tenue y gris . . . En su lugar había una calavera con los cuencos vacíos . . . (271)

Once again Trueba confuses the past with the present. A tyrant himself, he is bound in a sense by the tyranny of his own memory that is reduced to dust before his eyes. This delusion will be recalled later on when Trueba tries to rescue his granddaughter who becomes one of "los desaparecidos". His only alternative for helping her is through his former servant, now a prostitute, who maintains connections with the military rule. The complete transformation of state power finally hits Trueba when he realizes that his only tie to it is through a whorehouse. As the chapter's title suggests, this is "la hora de la verdad"—his own personal "patriarchal autumn".

While memory and imagination (or lack of it) victimize Trueba in a certain way, Alba ultimately develops them into skills as a means to survive and perhaps even prevail. Through the aid of her grandmother, she learns to keep herself and her memories alive by practicing an inner writing as a means of recording events:

> Clara trajo la idea salvadora de escribir con el pensamiento sin lápiz ni papel, para mantener la mente ocupada, evadirse de la perrera y vivir. Le surgió además que escribiera un testimonio que algún día podría servir para sacar a la luz el terrible secreto que estaba viviendo, para que el mundo se enterara del horror que ocurría paralelamente a la existencia apacible y ordenada de los que no querían saber, de los que podían tener la ilusión. (362)

It is this form of imaginative defiance, born out of desperation, that can make memory subversive—by keeping it alive and realizing its inextricable connection to the continuum of history, or, to quote a famous line: "*Never* to forget is a revolutionary act." Alba builds on her mother's and her grandmother's capacity to see destiny in their dreams. Throughout the novel, for instance, these women have predicted with certainty the earthquake, the coup, and the subsequent horror of the dictatorship. Whereas they have a kind of resignation to these apparently disconnected events, as if they have no control over them at the same time that they know they will occur, Alba finds herself in a position to *act* on what is happening to her. She must "act" in the sense of remembering or else the alternative is death. Through memory, she develops the knowledge that her family members foresaw and thus survives. As this knowledge becomes grounded in history, i.e., as history explains it, a basis for being prepared for the future is developed. Like "los inquilinos" whose experience has taught them that the fox always eats the hens, yet who none-the-less pass along tales, legends, and songs to the contrary, tradition does not always indicate how things will remain. There are always signs that must be analyzed so that the future does not take one by surprise, nor appear as some magically created destiny over which one has no control.

In other words, memory can be seen as a continuum or spectrum of history. At one end of this spectrum lies memory, and at the other clairvoyance or a kind of memory of the future. When the realization comes that this "clairvoyance" is not necessarily inexplicable or unrelated to history, then the strength to change one's "destiny" becomes a possibility. This explains in part Alba's transformation from a "mujercita burguesa" into a stronger individual translating the power of her mind into a tool for change. Indeed the act of "inner writing" itself suggests to Alba further possibilities for utilizing her knowledge to make the world remember what it chooses to ignore through the act of forgetting. As Umberto Eco has stated, " . . . el pasado no puede destruirse—su destrucción conduce al silencio—lo que hay que hacer es volver a visitarlo; con ironía, sin ingenuidad."[7]

It is in this light that we can examine Allende's novel, which in itself is a fine tool for remembering Chile's past, both remote and recent. We, as active readers, can take this testimony and use it as a way of never forgetting what happened to a family in a not too distant time and place, and also as a reminder of what could happen anywhere—even without precedent. Just imagine . . .

Notes

[1] It is important to recognize that Isabel Allende is the niece of the late president of Chile, Salvador Allende, who was killed in the CIA backed and the Pinochet led coup of 1973. I am interpreting her novel as dealing with the events leading up to the coup and the subsequent dictatorship it imposed.

[2] All page numbers written after quotes refer to Allende's novel. They are taken from the edition, *La casa de los espíritus*, Editorial Diana, México, 1985.

[3] Yates, Frances A., *The Art of Memory*, Routledge and Keegan, London, 1966.

[4] Ibid. page 10.

[5] Ibid. page 253.

[6] Ibid. page 95.

[7] Eco, Umberto. *Apostillas a El nombre de la rosa*, Editorial Lumen, Barcelona, 1985. p. 74.